Amphibians

These moist-skinned creatures were the first vertebrate hunters to colonize the land. Rarely venturing far from water, this group of animals include the familiar frog and toad, and the more secretive newt and salamander.

D0464513

Amphibians ruled the earth before any reptiles or mammals even existed. They were the first predatory vertebrates to adapt to life on land. The word amphibian is derived from the Greek words "amphi," meaning both, and "bios," meaning life. As their name suggests, amphibians are suited to both life on land and in the water. However, few of them venture far from water.

Amphibians are ectotherms and they are entirely reliant on environmental warmth to maintain bodily functions. Most species from temperate climates hibernate in winter to avoid lethally cold temperatures. Species from tropical climates aestivate to avoid lethally hot conditions.

Amphibians have delicate, moist skin that is covered with a protective mucus coating. This water-permeable skin offers very little protection from external toxins and chemicals, making amphibians very sensitive to their environment. They shed regularly and the nutritious shed skin

is generally eaten. Many amphibians display wonderful colors, either for the purpose of camouflage or as a warning to potential predators to show that they possess toxic skin.

All adult amphibians are predators. They feed mainly on spiders and insects and the larger species are even capable of eating small reptiles and mammals. Foods are swallowed rather than chewed. To aid in this process frogs, for example, possess tiny peg-like teeth to hold the prey before swallowing. As hunters, the eyes of amphibians are essential tools and need to be kept clean and wet. The eyes are covered with a fine membrane and blinking causes this membrane to wipe clean and moisten the eyeball in one action.

Amphibians generally lay soft, jelly-covered eggs into an aquatic environment. Thousands of eggs may be laid, but mortality is very high and fewer than one percent of these are likely to survive to breeding age in the wild. The eggs hatch into

◀ **The skeleton encases several organs found in all vertebrates—the liver, lungs, heart, and stomach. In this skeleton of the Common Frog, *Rana temporaria*, the large leg bones are clearly visible which, powered by strong muscles, enable frogs to leap great distances. Frogs also possess tiny, peg-like teeth to hold prey before it is swallowed.**

larvae, also known as tadpoles, and these eventually undergo a shape-changing metamorphosis into the adult form. These young adults then leave the water and adopt a more terrestrial lifestyle.

There are some species of amphibian, however, who do not follow these breeding rules. The unusual Axolotl is the classic exception. This creature has developed the capacity to breed while still in the larval, or tadpole, stage. This ability is called neotony.

Amphibians are in decline globally—pollution and habitat loss are the major factors. Since their skin is water-permeable, it offers them very little protection from man-made chemicals and the loss of breeding ponds results in populations being decimated. However, due to their high breeding capacity, it is possible to effectively repopulate areas with captive-bred stock over a relatively short period of time, providing the environmental conditions have improved.

▲ Smooth, moist skin is a characteristic of amphibians, such as this Fire Salamander. Unlike frogs, newts and salamanders are silent, unable to croak or call. They are also deaf, since they possess no ears. They are nocturnal creatures and actively hunt worms, slugs, and other invertebrate prey.

AMPHIBIAN CLASSIFICATION

Order	Description	No. of Species
ANURA	Frogs and toads. The best known of all the amphibians. Possess legs, but lose their tails once adult. This is the largest order, and contains some of the most widely kept amphibians.	2,600
URODELA	Newts and salamanders. Limbs and tails are both present in their adult forms. They do not have ears and sight is the major sense organ for finding food.	300
APODA	Caecilians—long worm-like amphibians. These are not covered in this book.	150

AXOLOTL

Ambystoma mexicanum

Found in the wild only in the canal system of the former Lake Xochimilcho in Mexico, these strange amphibians are easy to keep and make attractive, if unusual, aquatic pets.

Although officially an endangered species, Axolotls have been available from captive-bred stock since the 1830s. They are available in four color varieties. Black, or dark gray, is the most common coloring but albino, harlequin, and, more recently, a golden form, have all been captive bred and are available to the pet keeper. Growing to 12 in (30 cm), an Axolotl should live for 10–12 years in captivity. However, older specimens of some 20 years have been reported.

An unusual feature of Axolotls is that they do not go through a normal amphibian life cycle in which eggs laid in water by the adult hatch into tadpole-like "larvae," and then metamorphose into adults. At this stage the animal frequently leaves the water to take up a more terrestrial lifestyle. Axolotls have foregone the need to undergo metamorphosis. They remain in the aquatic, larval stage and reproduce without the need to become adult. The ability to do this is called neotony.

An Axolotl can only change into adult form when the hormone thyroxine is introduced into the diet or when there is an increase in the iodine levels in the water. The Axolotl gradually loses its gills, the tail reduces and, upon leaving the water, becomes a Mexican Salamander. Metamorphosis will not normally take place without this special treatment.

CREATING THE RIGHT ENVIRONMENT

A perfect home for a single Axolotl is an aquarium measuring 24 x 15 x 12 in (60 x 38 x 30 cm). The water should be aged tap water, i.e. left standing for 48 hours. Make sure the water is roughly neutral (pH 6.5–7.5) and maintained at a temperature of between 50–77°F (10–25°C). A heater is therefore not usually required. Water depth can be at least as deep as the length of your Axolotl, but specimens missing a limb or two may prefer shallower water until these have fully regenerated.

▶ **A healthy Axolotl will ideally have four limbs, a complete tail, and should hold itself stable in the water. Three branch-like gills on each side of the head enable the Axolotl to breathe underwater. The cooler the water, the smaller the gills, since more oxygen is present at lower temperatures.**

AMAZING FACT

The Axolotl is much studied due to its amazing powers of regeneration. A lost or damaged limb will regrow over a period of about 8 weeks. The new limb will be just as good as the old one and full flexibility will be retained. Occasionally, due to the extent of the original injury, the regenerated limb may regrow at an unusual angle.

◀ This aquarium provides spacious accommodation for a pair of Axolotls. It is decorated with pebbles and rocks, and the water is cleansed using an internal filter. The water level is kept deliberately low; it is about as deep as the Axolotl is long. Plastic plants are an attractive addition.

Axolotls will soon tear up a delicately planted aquarium, so they are best kept in a relatively plain setup. Gravel, pebbles, and even fine sand are suitable substrates. Adding larger rocks will provide visual appeal to the aquarium and will give your Axolotl some platforms upon which to rest. An external or internal filter is recommended to clean and aerate the water but it is not essential. Weekly cleaning of all the furnishings and partial changes of the water is an acceptable, although more time-consuming, alternative. Lighting the aquarium either from the side or from underneath makes a very attractive display.

Generally speaking, Axolotls are best housed separately, since they have a tendency to eat each others' limbs. These do regrow eventually, if not as perfectly as their originals. Keeping these creatures separately does not usually cause problems, since they seem totally unconcerned about the lack of company.

HANDLING

Axolotls are aquatic animals and do not like frequent handling. When necessary, they can be moved by scooping them into a net or by gently cradling them in the hands. Always transfer them between water of similar age and temperature so as not to cause them to go into shock.

▲ When your need to clean out your aquarium, your Axolotl can be gently cradled and lifted into temporary accommodation.

28

FOODS AND FEEDING

Axolotls are predators and they will eat a large variety of foods. Worms, crickets, small fish, fish pellets that sink or float, cubes of heart, or lean meat are all suitable foodstuffs—mine are especially partial to small freshwater shrimp. Food pieces should be kept to small, mouth-sized chunks because Axolotls cannot chew and will never learn to use a knife and fork!

▲ Requiring only a few feedings per week, the Axolotl is a popular and low maintenance aquatic pet.

A young Axolotl needs "training" to learn how to catch non-moving food, and long tweezers can be used to drop a piece of food onto its face. They suck in their prey and this violent motion can scare you from using your own fingers, but their teeth are very fine and will not hurt the adventurous keeper willing to hold a piece of food between finger and thumb. Axolotls can be fed every other day, with several mouthfuls of food given per sitting. Hungry Axolotls do seem to patrol their environment more than their well-fed companions, an indication that more food may be required. Uneaten food should be removed as soon as possible to minimize fouling.

BREEDING

Once your pet is 2 years old the sexes can be distinguished easily. Viewed from above, the male Axolotl's head is longer and narrower than the female's, his tail is longer, and the swelling by the cloaca is greater. Sexing is easiest when several specimens can be viewed together.

In captivity, the breeding season coincides with our winter and spring, when a change of temperature often triggers breeding behavior. This can be induced artificially by raising the water temperature to 72°F (22°C) for about a week or so, and then allowing it to drop quickly. With luck and a good diet, breeding behavior should follow. The female becomes attracted to the male's sweet excretions produced from his cloaca. She follows him around the aquarium, and they dance and swim around one another for some time. Eventually the male releases triangular jelly masses, called spermatophores, that sink to the bottom of the aquarium. The female is led over these masses until she takes some up into her cloacal opening. Some hours later she will start to spawn, and some 300–600 fertilized eggs are laid.

The egg masses are best reared separately from the parents to prevent them from being damaged or eaten. The eggs need good, but not too strong, aeration from a pump. After about two weeks at 68°F (20°C) the larvae will hatch and can then be fed on brine shrimp, tubiflex, powdered fish food, or other microscopic foods. As they grow, daphnia, glassworms, bloodworms, and mosquito larvae can also be consumed. Ample space is required to ensure a good survival rate for the hundreds of young, otherwise they will constantly snap and bite at each other.

AFRICAN CLAWED FROG

Xenopus laevis

These amphibians are totally aquatic and are noted for the absence of both tongue and eyelids. Their bodies have a somewhat flattened appearance and they possess powerful hind limbs.

Native to southern Africa, these clawed frogs grow to approximately 4–5 in (10–13 cm), and in captivity they can live to 15 years of age. They are powerful and agile swimmers with fully webbed hind limbs that are partially clawed. They are a simple species to keep, making them a popular choice for the novice keeper.

CREATING THE RIGHT ENVIRONMENT

Simple to maintain in captivity, these frogs have been bred for many generations under laboratory conditions. A 36 x 15 x 12 in (90 x 38 x 30 cm) aquarium, filled with water to a depth of about 5–8 in (13–20 cm) is adequate for a similar sized pair of frogs. To check for correct water depth, ensure that your frogs can reach the surface of the water to breathe while standing on the bottom of the tank. Keep water temperature at 68–77°F (20–25°C), using an aquarium heater if necessary, making sure that it is adequately protected from any possible damage by the frogs. To maintain water purity, gentle filtration using internal or external power filters is essential.

▲ Simple to keep, the African Clawed Frog is a popular, if unusual looking, amphibian.

To furnish your setup, use plants, rocks, pea-sized gravel, and you can even add flower pots for your frogs to hide in. Supplementary lighting is not required. Your frogs may take a little while to settle into their new home. If they frantically bash themselves against the sides of the tank when you approach, insert a dense, plastic plant at one end of the aquarium and allow the frogs to hide and gradually acclimatize to their new surroundings.

Dwarf Clawed Frog
Hymenochirus boettgeri

In the wild, these frogs from west Africa can be found in ditches and lakes at the edge of forests or cultivated areas. Measuring only $1^{1}/_{2}$ in (3.5 cm), they prefer an aquarium heated to 68–77°F (20–25°C) with a platform of floating plants to provide easy access to the water's surface. These small frogs breathe air, so access to the surface is essential. Suitable foods include daphnia, tubiflex, and small insects such as hatchling crickets and fruit flies.

HANDLING

These frogs are very difficult to handle. Coated with a protective slime, they slip through fingers even better than wet soap. If you need to move them, catch them in a net and transport them in plastic containers, without water, furnished with wet moss or wet foam pieces to keep your frog moist. Beware of transporting an African Clawed Frog in a bag of water because their claws may actually puncture the plastic.

FOODS AND FEEDING

A healthy African Clawed Frog will rarely refuse food, which it shuffles around with its long fingers. It will happily swim to the surface and take food from your fingers, which it then consumes underwater. Earthworms, small fish (e.g. minnow or guppy), waxworms, turtle and fish pellets are all agreeable foods these frogs. Like many amphibians they are easily overfed because they just don't know when to stop—in the wild they would never find a constant and abundant food source all the year round. Feed only as much as they will eat per 10-minute sitting, 3–4 times a week.

BREEDING

Males and females are easy to tell apart. The female is larger and more rounded and, when viewed from above, three flaps of skin next to the cloaca are visible.

Some environmental change seems to encourage spawning. Spraying the water surface or adding 2–3 in (5–8 cm) of water can start the process. Sometimes, however, the frogs spawn without any encouragement. On average, 1,000 eggs are laid per spawning and a single female can produce up to 10,000 per season. These should be removed immediately, to prevent the adults from eating them, and be kept in a shallow container until they hatch a couple of days later. The tadpoles have cannibalistic tendencies, so thin them out constantly, isolating faster growing specimens.

The organic soup required to feed the larvae may be purchased as a fish fry food, or by micro-mesh net dipping in a "good" pond (a chemical-free freshwater environment containing an abundance of micro-organisms).

ORIENTAL FIRE-BELLIED TOAD

Bombina orientalis

These hardy toads are ideal for the hobbyist. They are small, easy to keep, very active, and beautifully marked—easily one of the world's most attractive amphibians.

Native to cool mountain streams and rice paddies in China, Korea, and Siberia, these little toads can grow to about 2 in (5 cm) in length. Oriental Fire-bellied Toads have a bright green back with black markings, while their underparts are bright orange with black patches.

CREATING THE RIGHT ENVIRONMENT

Two options exist for keeping these toads in captivity. A large aquarium—36 x 15 x 12 in (90 x 38 x 30 cm)—which is ample space for three to four individuals (one male to three females); or, a moist woodland setting. In the former, the water should be maintained at a depth of 6–8 in (15–20 cm) and heated by a thermostatically controlled aquarium heater to a temperature of 74–77°F (23–25°C). Natural daylight is sufficient but a small spotlight or fluorescent tube may be used for aesthetic purposes. Real or plastic plants and gravel will enhance the display, and rocks or cork logs should be used to allow the frogs to climb out of the water.

Powerful rear leg muscles help to propel the toad towards its prey

The mottled body color serves as camouflage

The brightly colored underside warns predators of its unpleasant taste

▲ The small Oriental Fire-bellied Toad makes an excellent choice for a novice pet keeper.

Make sure the tank is securely covered but well ventilated—these toads are excellent escapees given the opportunity. An internal water filter should ease maintenance, but larger fecal pellets and uneaten or dead food are best removed with a siphon. The water should be partially changed every few weeks. Remember to wash all furnishings and gravel at the same time.

Alternatively, keep these toads in a moist woodland-style setup furnished only with mosses, logs, and a large, shallow water dish and maintain at 74–77°F (23–25°C). They will only need to be placed in a greater volume of water for breeding purposes.

HANDLING

Handling a happy toad is safe but not recommended regularly, nor is it even necessary. Like other amphibians, these toads contain known toxins and you should not handle them if you have cuts on your skin. When threatened, they lie flat and curl all their fingers and toes above their backs. This shows any predator that they are brightly colored and potentially toxic. If actually attacked, an acrid, white fluid can ooze from pores on the back—this is toxic if swallowed. The threat display and release of toxins is rarely seen and should not deter you from acquiring this species.

FOODS AND FEEDING

These little toads feed well, and prefer live insect prey—crickets, grasshoppers, spiders, flies, etc. They feed mainly on land and will soon learn to come to your fingers when offered food. Feed as much as will be eaten 2–3 times a week and add vitamin supplements regularly. The superb coloration of Oriental Fire-bellied Toads will fade with captive-bred offspring unless coloring agents are provided (found in prepared fish foods and flakes). The toads obtain these naturally by eating a multitude of tiny wild foods.

BREEDING

Spring is the most likely time for these toads to start calling. The male is particularly noisy and his constant "croaking" should attract a willing female. Spawning will occur within 8–24 hours of mating, probably during the night. Up to 200 eggs may be laid per spawning, singularly or in clumps. Eggs should be transferred to a rearing container filled with similarly aged and warmed water. The 0.08 in (2 mm) eggs will hatch within a few days.

Once the larvae have absorbed their yolk sacs, they will be ready to start feeding. Finely chopped tubiflex, hatchling crickets, and aquarium fry-food can all be given. Remove waste matter regularly. About 3 weeks after hatching the toads are ready to leave the water for the first time. They will be mature enough to breed at about 12 months.

Giant Toad
Bufo marinus

This is the largest known species of toad, measuring 10 in (25 cm). Native to South and Central America and the Caribbean, these toads have, however, become established in Florida and they gather under lights at night to eat insects. They are ravenous feeders and will eat almost any animal they can fit into their mouths. This terrestrial species can become very tame. They require a large vivarium—36 x 15 x 12 in (90 x 38 x 30 cm)—with temperatures of 68–77°F (20–25°C). The toxin from the parotid glands behind the eyes is strong enough to make an attacking dog sick.

FIRE SALAMANDER

Salamandra salamandra

These secretive creatures are mainly nocturnal, spending the day hidden under loose rocks or inside old rodent burrows. A cool and moist, mossy forest floor is their ideal habitat.

Highly variable in patterning, the bright yellow coloration of the Fire Salamander is very striking and you are highly unlikely to mistake it for any other creature.

Their natural range extends through central and southern Europe into North Africa and western Asia. They are easy to keep in captivity and can grow to 12 in (30 cm) in length.

The eye is able to detect even static prey

parotid glands

▲ Secretive and nocturnal, this salamander makes a fascinating pet.

The skin of a healthy salamander shoud be bright and shiny

CREATING THE RIGHT ENVIRONMENT

Fire Salamanders are very easy to accommodate. However, they are quite territorial and it may be easier to house individuals separately. A vivarium measuring 36 x 15 x 12 in (90 x 38 x 30 cm) or 48 x 15 x 12 in (120 x 38 x 30 cm) provides spacious living quarters and is ideal for a single specimen or a pair. If you do decide to keep a small group, provide them with plenty of hiding places and adequate food to minimize competition.

Furnish your vivarium with several inches of peat moss and leaves to provide a cool, damp base, and add some cork or a small rotting log to provide hiding places. A shallow dish sunk into the ground is useful; salamanders drown very easily, so keep the water shallow and use pebbles or a slope to ensure the salamander can easily climb out. Mist spray your pets regularly.

Fire Salamanders, like some other amphibians, are visually aware and set up "home" at a regular site. When cleaning out vivaria, it helps to replace some of the "landmark" objects in their original spots to prevent confusing your pet.

These amphibians like cool, low-light conditions, 60–68°F (15–20°C), so heating is not usually required, but use a thermometer as a guide. Salamanders will look for suitable habitats if necessary. During my teens my Fire Salamander escaped. Over a year later my father was re-plumbing the bathroom and it re-emerged, giving him quite a shock. It had found suitably damp conditions and probably survived on house spiders, pill bugs, and stray worms.

HANDLING

The bright colors of the salamander serve as a warning to any potential predator. Many creatures learn very quickly that these rubbery amphibians ooze toxic, milky secretions from their skin when bitten or aggravated. Therefore great care should be taken when handling your pet salamander. Personally I have never heard of any unhappy incidents involving salamanders, but it is best to be aware of this unpleasant defense mechanism. Enjoy your salamander but, as with all animals, treat it with respect.

FOODS AND FEEDING

If fed at a regular time, your salamander will learn to emerge from hiding in anticipation of food. These amphibians eat a range of live foods. As a terrestrial species, climbing foods, such as grasshoppers are best ignored. Slugs, spiders, and earthworms, which remain at the salamander's level, are by far the most suitable foodstuffs.

Be very careful when feeding several salamanders at the same time because they are more than likely to fight over the same bit of food. As a simple rule, feed your pet salamander as much as will be eaten at a single sitting, 2–3 times per week. Without distressing your salamanders too much by leaving excess live food crawling all over them, leave a few worms and insects loose in the vivarium to be eaten or found at their leisure.

BREEDING

Fire Salamanders are frequently bred in captivity, usually during the spring and early summer. Courtship occurs on land and involves the male carrying the female around, often for several hours, on his back. After stimulation of her cloacal region, the female picks up a deposited spermatophore. At this time the female needs access to shallow water.

She will eventually bear up to 70 well-formed larvae direct into the water—ensure that the water is filtered gently. These larvae have developed inside the female's body from eggs, and like Axolotl larvae, feed on tiny organisms in the water, known as infusoria. The larvae should be transferred to a rearing container to prevent the adults from eating their offspring. Some 3–5 months later metamorphosis will take place; at this stage the gills will reduce as the young start to breathe oxygen. In some populations the female develops the larvae for longer inside her body and gives birth to fully developed juveniles, already colored with the yellow blotches and stripes.

Tiger Salamander
Ambystoma tigrinum

These attractive salamanders are native to North America. Growing to 13 in (33 cm), they are the largest of the terrestrial salamanders. Coloring tends to be variable, ranging from black to brown, with bright spots or blotches of light gray. They tame easily and enjoy eating live foods such as worms and snails. Living conditions should be similar to those of the Fire Salamander, with an ideal temperature range of 60–74°F (15–23°C).

RED-SPOTTED NEWT

Notophthalmus v. viridescens

Native to eastern North America, these charming and attractive newts make an ideal introduction to the world of tailed amphibians.

Red-spotted Newts go through a "red eft" stage upon metamorphosis. These juveniles are usually red with black dots on their backs and lead a terrestrial lifestyle. Once adult, their skin becomes brown and is covered in red spots, encircled with a black border. At this stage, they return to the water to live and breed. Easy to maintain, these newts grow to a length of 4 in (10 cm) and live for 4–6 years.

CREATING THE RIGHT ENVIRONMENT

The habitat requirements of these newts change as they mature. Metamorphosed juveniles are terrestrial but adults are mostly aquatic. The "red efts" take 2–3 years to mature and only then will they return permanently to the water as adults. Several newts may be accommodated in a 24 x 15 x 12 in (60 x 38 x 30 cm) aquarium, but one measuring 36 x 15 x 12 in (90 x 38 x 30 cm)

would give you more scope to create a semi-aquatic setup to accommodate both the aquatic and terrestrial stages of a newt's life cycle.

A well-planned vivarium consists of a densely planted aquatic region, with a water depth of 6–9 in (15–23 cm), and a large platform, or cork logs wedged or stuck to the inside of the tank, to create a land area. Sloping branches or rocks provide easy access to the water.

Cover the land area with leaf litter, wood chips, moss, and pieces of log or cork for your juvenile to utilize as living and hunting spaces. They do not appreciate damp and stale conditions or habitats that are too dry, so humidity should be moderate, say around 40–50%. Full-spectrum lighting may enhance the look of your setup but it is not vital for newt health—good natural daylight is sufficient; however, do not place in direct sunlight.

Mucus glands are located all over the body and produce a slimy secretion to protect the skin and keep it moist

Supported by a very delicate skeleton, the tiny body makes it an unsuitable pet for regular handling

The tail makes up half of the overall body length

▲ **Red-spotted Newts are agile and fast hunters of the water's edge.**

Northern Crested Newt
Triturus cristatus

These newts are found in Britain and grow to approximately 6 ½ in (17 cm) in length. Their numbers are declining in the wild due to habitat loss, so they are protected by law and cannot be collected from the wild or have their habitats destroyed. Those available are from captive-bred stocks and are better adapted to captivity than wild-caught salamanders.

Red-spotted Newts are content to live at room temperature, 65°F (18°C). The environment should not become too hot and the maximum recommended temperature is 72°F (22°C). Use an external power filter for optimum water quality. Add plants to the water to provide an attractive environment for your newts. Plastic plants are more hygienic because they do not rot. If you wish to use real plants, use fluorescent lighting to encourage good plant growth.

▲ **These newts will patrol the vivarium searching for small insects, looking both above and below the water's surface.**

HANDLING

These newts produce toxic skin secretions, making them unpalatable to many predators. Although these toxins will not make you ill, it is best to handle your newt as little as possible. If you do need to handle them, do take care since they are small, which means they must be handled with care to avoid an injury.

FOODS AND FEEDING

Terrestrial efts will hunt small live foods such as young crickets, waxmoth larvae, fruit flies, earthworms, spiders and beetles. Aquatic adults hunt among the plants and search out daphnia, mosquito larvae, bloodworm, and other aquatic micro-organisms, many of which can be purchased at pet stores. Smaller live foods (i.e., crickets and fruit flies) may also be dropped onto the water surface. Offer food on a regular basis and leave some live foods in the vivarium for your newts to hunt.

BREEDING

Males actively court the females in water during springtime. Invisible scents, called pheromones, are produced by the male's cloacal glands and these are directed toward a potential mate using the tail. Eventually, a receptive female will pick up the spermatophore directly into her cloacal region. A few weeks later she will lay up to 400 individual eggs. These hatch in about 4–8 weeks and the tiny larvae begin to feed on suspended microorganisms for about 3 months. During this time they will have grown from ½ in (1 cm) to 2 in (4.5 cm) in length and will be ready to undergo metamorphosis.

TREE FROGS

Family: Hylidae

Tree frogs are the acrobats of the amphibian world. Possessing comical swollen pads on their digits, these lively creatures can reach parts of the vivarium other frogs can only dream about.

Found in warmer climates across the globe, tree frogs are often extremely colorful and several species are successfully kept and bred by herpetologists. As their name suggests, the majority of tree frogs are arboreal, spending most of their time off the ground in plants and trees. Any vertical surface may be climbed, even glass. Having found a suitable spot, they will curl their forelimbs and legs close in to the body and rest, tucked away like this all day, awaiting night fall or more crepuscular conditions.

WHITE'S TREE FROG
Litoria caerulea

Large, chubby, and with a permanent smiling expression, the White's or Dumpy Tree Frog is by far the most common pet tree frog. Native to north east Australia and New Guinea, these arboreal frogs live in rainforest-type habitats. When adult, this species can reach a length of 2–4 in (5–10 cm) and can live for up to 15 years. Their color can vary from dark olive to vibrant green.

CREATING THE RIGHT ENVIRONMENT
Tall vivaria are required for most tree frogs and White's are no exception. A vivarium measuring 24 x 18 x 12 in (60 x 45 x 30 cm) and filled with robust branches, plants, and furnishings is ideal for one or two adults. A substrate of moss, bark chips, stones and pebbles is recommended.

A large bowl of water should be offered and daily mist spraying is beneficial. However, make sure there is a reasonable amount of ventilation to prevent excess dampness. Keep the temperature between 77–86°F (25–30°C) during the day and reduce slightly at night. If you plan to keep more than one tree frog, make sure that individuals are of the same size to prevent cannibalism.

HANDLING
While individual characters vary, most White's tolerate handling well. Ensure that your hands are moist to prevent any damage to their delicate skin. Sometimes, when your frog is nervous or exercising, a small cupful of liquid can be expelled from the anus. This liquid is often assumed to be urine, but it is only water.

▲ **This is one of the easiest species of tree frog to handle. The large toe pads feel sticky and help this species to grip your hand securely.**

▶ **This trio of White's Tree Frogs show a range of coloration. Possessing a fixed smiling expression, this greedy species grows rapidly and requires sturdy furnishings to support its weight.**

FOODS AND FEEDING

These frogs are quite capable of eating small dead vertebrates, such as other frogs, lizards, and pinkies, but they will be just as happy to eat live foods such as large grasshoppers, big crickets, and earthworms. Depending on the size of your pet, feed 3–5 insects to each frog per sitting, 2–3 times per week.

BREEDING

A separate aquarium measuring 24 x 15 x 12 in (60 x 38 x 30 cm), with a water depth of a few inches at 77°F (25°C), is needed to attempt breeding. Once your frogs are in their new environment, a simulation of approaching rains will encourage mating. Try reducing humidity to 40–60% and the temperature to 65–68°F (18–20°C) for a week or so. Then gradually raise the humidity to 90% and the temperature to 77–86°F (25–30°C) and spray frequently with water to imitate rainfall.

It is essential that the frogs can easily enter and leave the pool at will. A sturdy branch or rock positioned against the edge of the water area will be sufficient. Between 200–300 eggs are laid as spawn and these will hatch in approximately 24 hours. Within 4–6 weeks the larvae, or tadpoles, will have grown sufficiently to trigger the process of metamorphosis. The young frogs will grow rapidly and should be separated into smaller groups to prevent overcrowding. They will mature between 1–2 years of age.

GREEN TREE FROG
Hyla cinerea

In the wild this species is found in the forests and meadows of the southwest states. Their bright green bodies are quite slender and they have a cream stripe running down each side of the body. Measuring only $1^1/_2$–$2^1/_2$ in (4–6 cm), they are ideal for keeping in a vivarium; indeed, they are one of the most popular types of tree frog available to the hobbyist.

CREATING THE RIGHT ENVIRONMENT

A semi-moist vivarium suits these tree frogs. Height is essential and three or four specimens may be housed in a vivarium measuring 24 x 18 x 12 in (60 x 46 x 30 cm). During spring and summer, maintain at a temperature of 65–77°F (18–25°C), cooling to 54–65°F (12–18°C) at night. Cover the land area with mosses, wood chips, twigs, and leaves and, even out of breeding season, a water dish should be available at all times. Ideally, the ground area should be divided into three parts land and one part water.

European Tree Frog
Hyla arborea

The European species is fairly rounded and has a brown stripe running through the eye and along its flanks. This specimen (above) has an unusual yellow coloration. They are hardier than the Green Tree Frog and grow to a length of 2 in (5 cm). Care conditions are identical to that of the Green Tree Frog. If you wish, you may keep them together with anoles in a community-type setup.

Insert branches or cork logs to provide climbing opportunities. Ferns or robust Philodendron plants should also be considered.

Avoid using unprotected incandescent light or spotlights because the light will not encourage activity and tree frogs often injure themselves fatally when leaping onto a hot light bulb. Heat pads and protected heaters are fine. A full-spectrum light tube should be provided since tree frogs benefit from exposure to UV rays.

HANDLING

This species is quite easy to handle but, again, ensure that your hands are wet. Green Tree Frogs tame relatively quickly as they respond well to feeding from the hand.

FOODS AND FEEDING

Many tree frogs prefer flying foods; blue bottles and house flies excite them into activity and provide much amusement for the observer. Most live foods, such as crickets, flies, locust hoppers, and worms will be accepted. Feed your Greens 2–3 times per week; as a general rule they eat more in spring and summer than in winter.

BREEDING

Green Tree Frogs are most likely to breed after a period of over-wintering or hibernation, followed by moving to larger quarters supplied with greater amounts of water. The short breeding season occurs around April and May, and the males are very loud when calling. After amplexus, the coupling pair enter the water. The eggs are fertilized by the male as they

▲ **This Green Tree Frog is resting on a piece of cork bark ready to leap at prey.**

leave the female's body and several clumps of 100–300 eggs are deposited among the water plants. Transfer these eggs to shallow rearing containers where the water is filtered, aerated, and kept at about 68°F (20°C).

Several days later the larvae, or tadpoles, hatch and should be fed on microscopic organisms and fine powdered fish food. Metamorphosis takes place about a month later and the froglets, measuring $1/2$–$3/4$ in (1–2 cm) and brown or green in color, are ready for a more terrestrial life. They mature at 2–3 years.

AMAZING FACT

Most temperate amphibians hibernate to avoid lethally cold winters. Upon emerging in spring, most species will be eager to breed. Replicate this rest period by cooling your frogs gradually to 41–50°F (5–10°C). You will find that even just a few weeks at reduced temperatures will encourage your pets to breed once they are warmed up again. Before trying this for yourself, ask a breeder or dealer for more advice.

▲ Less hardy than other tree frogs, the Red-eyed is a popular and visually stunning amphibian pet.

RED-EYED TREE FROG
Agalychnis callidryas

One of the most striking of all amphibians, this tree frog has bright red eyes, orange feet, and blue and white stripes on its flanks. They are frequently available from captive-bred stocks and are best purchased when approximately 1/2–1 in (1–2 cm) in length, growing to 3 in (8 cm) when adult. Starting with young healthy specimens seems the best approach because they should settle in fairly quickly within the conditions you are providing.

CREATING THE RIGHT ENVIRONMENT

Tall vivaria, measuring 18 x 24 x 12 in (45 x 60 x 30 cm), furnished with real plants and branches, should be provided for these wonderful frogs. Attaining the correct balance of humidity, temperature, and ventilation is important for the successful care of these and, indeed, most vivarium pets. These creatures prefer 50–80% humidity and a daytime temperature of 77–86°F (25–30°C), dropping to approximately 68°F (20°C) at night when they become active. Make sure ventilation is adequate.

A water bowl must be available at all times and should be cleaned every other day because these, and other amphibians, absorb water into the bladder—dirty water may often lead to fatal infections. A full-spectrum light source benefits most species and also encourages good plant growth.

HANDLING

These bright frogs tend to be slow moving and ponderous by nature. They are nocturnal and when at rest during the day the bright colors are completely concealed from view by the foliage. Handle cautiously, and only when necessary, because their skin is extremely delicate—it is far better to enjoy this species visually. If you need to move them, wait until they are at rest on a leaf and then place them and the leaf in a small tub with air holes. Keep them warm and moist.

FOODS AND FEEDING

Red-eyed Tree Frogs are particularly fond of flying foods such as flies and moths, but crickets and other live foods of suitable size can also be offered. Dust the food with multi-vitamins and give each frog as much as will be eaten at each sitting, 2–3 times per week.

BREEDING

In the wild, these arboreal frogs breed in bushes, shrubs, and trees that overhang water. Eggs are laid in a frothy mass on leaves and the tadpoles, on feeling rain, drop from the leaf into the water below. To trigger breeding in captivity, try the simulation technique used for the White's Tree Frog. A large bowl or small pool of water will be necessary. Tiny froglets require small insect foods dusted with supplements to ensure healthy development.

▲ **Small and delicate amphibians require careful handling. Red-eyed Tree Frogs are best left in their vivaria and handled only when necessary.**

Reptiles 1
Lizards and Tortoises

Reptiles are primitive vertebrates that have been around for millions of years. Their waterproof, scaly skin enables them to thrive in a variety of habitats. This group of animals includes lizards and tortoises.

The term herpetology, the study of reptiles and amphibians, is derived from the Greek word "herpeton," which means a creeping animal. Indeed, both lizards and tortoises do crawl, but the extent of this type of behavior is essentially controlled by their need to thermoregulate.

Unlike mammals, which utilize food to maintain a steady internal temperature, the temperature of a reptile is entirely dependent on its external environment. Reptiles need to bask in the sun or sit upon warm ground when they are cold and, conversely, they must retreat into shaded areas if they are too hot to avoid fatal overheating. The ability to darken or lighten their skin also helps this process—darker skin absorbs heat, while lighter skin reflects it. Reptiles are often misleadingly referred to as "cold-blooded" animals, but during basking their blood may reach temperatures that are warmer than that of a human.

During hot and cold seasons, when temperatures reach extreme levels, reptiles will become inactive. Aestivation and hibernation are the terms used to describe this process, whereby the metabolism is greatly reduced and reptiles enter a torpid, inactive state. Aestivation occurs in tropical areas and hibernation takes place in temperate regions.

Reptile skin is effectively watertight because it is covered by protective scales. In some species, like the chelonia, these scales are enlarged and contain bony plates which, along with flattened and fused vertebrae, form the shell. Scales are formed from an outer layer of dead skin; in order for the enclosed animal to grow, this layer is shed or sloughed off regularly and renewed from underneath. Many lizards eat this recyclable material. The skin of reptiles may appear to be shiny but it is never slimy. Reptiles do not sweat and, unlike mammals, they do not have sebaceous glands.

Most species eat a variety of foodstuffs but generally they consume more animal matter than plant material. Several lizards have even developed unique predatory techniques to lure prey. For example, the long tongue of the chameleon and the insect-luring tail of many species of skink.

The majority of lizards, and all chelonia, are egg layers. The eggs may be deposited into leaf litter, buried in the ground, or even stuck to tree bark. Some eggs have a hard shell while others have a leathery, pliable composition. Once eggs are laid, they are incubated. Reptile young are always born, or hatch, as miniature replicas of their parents—no metamorphic stage exists as it does in amphibians.

▲ **Tortoises are long-lived reptiles, with some living to over 100 years of age.**

◀ Thousands of lizards and tortoises are bred in captivity for the pet trade, greatly improving the quality and suitability of specimens for the enthusiast.

REPTILE CLASSIFICATION

Order	Description	No. of Species
SQUAMATA	Lizards and snakes. This group of reptiles is split into two sub-orders, the Sauria (lizards) and Serpentes (snakes). Lizards usually possess four legs, a long tail, and moving eyelids, while snakes are limbless and have fused eyelids.	5,150
CHELONIA	Tortoises and turtles. These creatures possess a bony shell made of horny plates that enclose their soft body. Terrestrial and aquatic forms exist.	230
CROCODILIA	Alligators, crocodiles, and gharials. These are large predatory reptiles that live in or near water. If kept in captivity, crocodilians must be licensed.	21
RHYNCHOCEPHALIA	Tuatara. This lizard-like reptile evolved before the dinosaurs and is the sole survivor of its order. It is an endangered species found only on a few islands off New Zealand.	1

LEOPARD GECKO

Eublepharis macularius

These velvet-skinned lizards are marked as their name suggests, like a leopard, and are found in the harsh, arid habitats of north-western India and Pakistan.

Leopard Geckos are members of the Gekkonidae family. Most members of this family are noted for their climbing abilities. Fine hair-like structures of specially modified scales enable them to climb glass or walk across a ceiling. Leopard Geckos, however, are a ground-dwelling species, which use their sharp claws for digging and for clambering about on rocks and logs. Fully grown adults measure 8–9 in (20–22 cm). The young, thousands of which are bred each year for hobbyists, are generally purchased when they are a few months old and 3–4 in (7–10 cm) in length. These geckos can live for up to 20 years in captivity.

▲ The subtle differences of pattern and coloring in a reptile population are called phases—the light and dark phases for this gecko are shown here.

In their natural habitat, different Leopard Gecko populations show some variety in color strength and patterning. These subtle differences continue to be present in the captive-bred population and two phases are commonly seen. A third phase—showing a chocolate coloration—is gaining popularity in some parts of the country.

CREATING THE RIGHT ENVIRONMENT

The Leopard Gecko's natural habitat is arid and desert-like. To simulate this environment and to provide all the essentials for survival, your set-up needs to include the following: several shelters in which to sleep, hunt, and remain unobserved; a shallow water dish for drinking; and an area that can be sprayed regularly to provide a humid micro-climate. The latter ensures that your lizard does not dehydrate and helps to facilitate periodic skin shedding.

Leopard Geckos will thrive at temperatures between 80–90°F (27–32°C). A well-designed vivarium should provide your gecko with a hot spot and various cooler areas within this range to allow it to thermoregulate effectively. Use a undertank heater at one end of the vivarium. The temperature may drop to 70°F (21°C) at night without any ill effect. These geckos are nocturnal, so no overhead light bulbs or ultra-violet light is necessary.

Washed sand, wood chips, rounded gravel, and pebbles can all be used as a base medium or substrate. Cork bark, cactus skeleton, or other suitable material can be stacked or glued together to provide shelters. Live succulent plants, except cactus, may be introduced to good effect—simply bury the pot into the substrate.

Geckos are very clean and will choose one spot in their vivarium to use as a toilet. The dry droppings should be removed regularly. If housing a single specimen, your setup should be cleaned out completely once every 2–3 months—make sure the vivarium, rocks, and plastic plants are also cleaned and disinfected. Your pet lizard must be housed in temporary accommodation while its home undergoes a thorough cleaning.

A 24 x 12 x 15 in (60 x 30 x 38 cm) vivarium provides ample space for a single specimen, while a 36 x 12 x 15 in (90 x 30 x 38 cm) vivarium would be suitable for a trio. Professional breeders often keep adults, and rear juveniles, in considerably smaller containers.

Ideally, your Leopard Geckos should be housed separately, where there is no competition for food or prime resting sites, and they will not be

A plump tail is a sign of a healthy, well-fed Leopard Gecko. The tail acts as a depository for stored fats, helping the lizard to survive periods of drought or when food is scarce

A healthy Leopard Gecko has bright eyes and appears clean, alert, and can hold its body off the ground when walking

Avoid emaciated, dull-looking specimens with shed skin still attached to the body

Leopard Geckos are ground dwelling. Unlike other geckos they lack adhesive pads on their digits

This gecko is $8^{1}/_{2}$ in (22 cm) long—an average size for an adult

▲ All pet Leopard Geckos are bred in captivity. One of the best pet reptiles in the world, these lizards are clean, attractive, and very easy to keep.

49

harassed by any other individual. It is very important not to keep males together because the strongest and most established specimens will bully smaller, weaker animals. Females can be kept together and a small colony of, say, four females and one male is also fine. One simple rule for colonies—the more space and hiding places you provide, the less any one individual will be harassed or become subordinate. Alternatively, you could keep a pair, housed separately, only introducing them for breeding for short periods, of a day or so, at a time.

HANDLING

Leopard Geckos tolerate handling well but, like any pet, handling should be done with care, consideration, and patience. Sitting down while holding your pet will ensure that there is less likelihood of injury if it jumps out of your hand or is dropped. The best time to start taming your lizard is when it is still young. Handle for short, regular periods to show the reptile that you pose no threat to its safety—offer some food by hand as a possible reward.

▼ Unlike most geckos, this species has moveable eyelids that enable it to blink. This helps to keep the eye free of sand and dirt.

▲ A small plastic container is ideal as a hide box. Containing vermiculite, it is likely to be utilized by a female looking for an egg laying site.

FOODS AND FEEDING

Leopard Geckos should eat every other day or so. They may be fed most small to medium live foods, such as crickets, a few of which should always be available within the vivarium for the geckos to stalk. A young adult will eat, on average, 5–6 insects at a sitting, several times a week. Supply water in a very shallow dish, positioned level with the ground.

BREEDING

Leopard Geckos breed well in captivity. You may wish to try this yourself, but make sure that you have a separate home ready for your new offspring. Mating usually occurs unseen in a covered area, and the first signs of a successful coupling is the female's noticeably swollen belly. Each female can lay several clutches of 2 eggs per year. She will try to find a damp and secure spot to lay and bury her eggs, probably under the shelter or among plastic plants heaped on the ground. Try to encourage her to lay her eggs in a suitable spot—an upturned plastic container, with a hole cut in one side, and filled with dampened sphagnum moss, is ideal. Otherwise check the vivarium regularly.

The two eggs, being a standard clutch for most geckos, should be transferred to an incubator to prevent desiccation. Unlike many bird eggs, reptile eggs should not be turned—simply place in the incubating medium (I use vermiculite) and cover. Provide airflow but keep humidity at 70–80% and maintain a temperature of 86°F (30°C).

The incubating eggs should be checked on a regular basis—very shriveled or moldy ones should be removed to avoid contaminating healthy eggs. A white but slightly indented egg needs a higher humidity level. The young will hatch after 6–12 weeks. The juveniles are marked with yellow and black bands that will gradually break up into the familiar adult markings. They should be housed in small rearing containers, separately if possible. If kept communally, you must provide several hiding places and water dishes, removing the more dominant individuals once they begin to harass others. A daily misting will ensure good skin condition and will ease frequent shedding as the juveniles grow. Small crickets and waxworms are ideal first foods—geckos also adore small spiders. All foodstuffs should be lightly dusted with a multivitamin and mineral supplement.

Day Geckos
Phelsuma sp

Like wonderful living jewels, these diurnal lizards look like they have just had a fight in a paint shop. Day Geckos are native to tropical Madagascar, Mauritius, the Seychelles, and other islands in the Indian Ocean. The majority are arboreal and are 4–6 in (10–15 cm) in length.

Day Geckos are ideal for a tall, preferably planted, humid vivarium and will remain active for most of the day. Accommodation measuring 24 x 18 x 12 in (60 x 45 x 30 cm) is suitable for 2–3 specimens. Full-spectrum fluorescent lighting is recommended for Day Geckos and to maintain a visually stunning, planted vivarium. Do not handle the gecko—its skin tears at the lightest touch. The temperature should be maintained at between 77–90°F (25–32°C) using a spotlight—humid, but not stagnant air—with good ventilation.

As well as eating live foods, such as crickets, these reptiles enjoy licking fruit, nectar, or sap from tropical plants. An upside-down jam jar lid, or bottle top, is ideal for serving vitamin/mineral enhanced honey, jam, or small fruit pieces, such as mango or grape. They prefer drinking from droplets on leaves, so mist once a day.

AMAZING FACT

The incubating temperature of many reptile eggs will dictate the sex of the hatchling. At 86°F (30°C) the sexes are likely to be mixed. At lower temperatures, 77–82°F (25–28°C), the majority of young are likely to be female. Raising the temperature to 90°F (32°C) should produce males.

GREEN ANOLE

Anolis carolinensis

Once called American Chameleons, these delightful green lizards are fascinating to watch—they are very active and regularly display their colorful throat fans.

Native to the southern United States, Central America, and the Caribbean, Green Anoles are one of the most commonly kept lizards in the world. They can often be found on walls, fences, bushes, and shrubs in gardens and other man-made settlements.

These diurnal tree lizards were once called American Chameleons. They measure 5–8 in (13–20 cm) in length and the tail, essential for balancing, makes up two-thirds of their total length. An average life expectancy of 3–5 years is typical.

Males are very territorial and aggressive to one another. Much of their time is spent displaying ownership of a particular area, usually with much head bobbing and extension of their colorful throat fan, or dewlap.

CREATING THE RIGHT ENVIRONMENT

These lizards need a tall vivarium with a moist environment, with an ideal daytime temperature range of 74–86°F (23–30°C), which may drop to 68°F (20°C) at night. At least one basking spotlight and a full spectrum light are needed to assist the healthy development of these reptiles. The spot and fluorescent lights are also necessary to maintain healthy growth of the real plants that should be provided in a vivarium that is as tall and as large as possible.

For a harem of four females and one male, I would suggest a vivarium measuring at least 36 x 24 x 12 in (90 x 60 x 30 cm). At least two basking spots are needed and many suitable territories should be created. Provide some branches or logs and a suitable substrate, such as potting compost covered with a layer of wood chips or leaf litter. Males should be housed separately if a large vivarium is not available.

Cleaning will be largely aesthetic, mainly to remove visible droppings from leaves and the sides of the vivarium. Soiled areas of compost

This adult male is more brightly colored than the female of the species. Only the males display, using their colorful throat fans, or dewlaps

The long snout enables females to push their eggs into soil for safe incubation

Brown Anole
Anolis sagrei

Approximately 300 species and subspecies of anoles are recognized and all have similar requirements to the Green Anole. Dewlap colors are variable, ranging from yellow with an orange spot to orange or red. Many species lay up to four eggs, often in bromeliad leaf rosettes. Anoles are welcomed in homes and gardens because they eat many insect pests. The other common anole available to the pet keeper is the Brown Anole, *Anolis sagrei*. They can be kept alongside Green Anoles but the Browns are slightly more terrestrial in their habit, and less likely to use the maximum height of the vivarium.

The color of these lizards can change from green to brown. Changes are the result of changes in mood, temperature, light intensity, and stress as much as for camouflage purposes

▲ Anoles are very active lizards. They can run fast on plant foliage and leap readily from one spot to another.

can easily be scooped out. A planted vivarium will need tending like a garden rather than requiring the thorough cleaning necessary for a more artificial setup that uses, say, plastic plants and cork logs.

HANDLING
Although fast and able to leap about, an anole will learn to sit on your hand in its cage in exchange for a tasty treat. These small and delicate lizards need a gentle touch. Allowing your anole to climb onto your hand is less stressful for the lizard, but be careful as it is likely to escape. If you wish to move your pet, grip it firmly but gently in the hand.

FOODS AND FEEDING
These insectivores will eat any small to medium live insect foods. Mealworms should be avoided because many will pass through these reptiles undigested. Feed at least twice weekly by adding several live insects into the vivarium, watching to ensure that every occupant gets at least two insects per feeding. A small surplus amount of live food may be present in the vivarium at all times. You will soon familiarize yourself with when, and how often, your anoles need feeding by the size of their bellies and general behavior.

Mist spraying once a day or so is essential because they prefer to drink water droplets from leaves rather than still water from a bowl. The vivarium should not become too wet, however, because the environment will become stagnant.

BREEDING
Once you establish a group of these lizards and they are well fed and happy, breeding is sure to follow. One or two eggs are laid about two weeks after mating. These will be buried by the female, or nosed into the compost in a warm and damp area, frequently around the pot or roots of a climbing plant, such as Philodendron.

BEARDED DRAGONS

Pogona vitticeps

Native to Australia, these heavy-bodied lizards are partly arboreal and enjoy basking on tree stumps and garden fences. They have appealing characters and are easy to keep in a vivarium.

Growing to 16–24 in (40–60 cm), Bearded Dragons are a social species and interesting behavior, such as courtship, recognition, threat, and appeasement, may all be observed within the vivarium. Spiky, elongated scales, or "beard," cover the huge throat pouch, and can be extended when a Bearded Dragon feels threatened, making an open mouth and inflated body an effective threat posture.

Temperatures should reach 82–104°F (28–40°C) at the hottest spot in the vivarium during the day, but can reduce to 68°F (20°C) during the night. For this diurnal species, 12 hours of daylight is sufficient and a dark rest period is essential for sleep. A large, clean water dish should be available at all times for bathing, and your Bearded Dragon will enjoy an occasional mist spraying.

CREATING THE RIGHT ENVIRONMENT

A dry woodland, or desert-style vivarium measuring 30 x 20 x 30 in (76 x 51 x 76 cm) is suitable for an adult pair or trio of Bearded Dragons. Insert cork logs or rocks for climbing on or burrowing under and cover the vivarium floor with bark chips or sand. Add leaves and pine cones, or live succulents, to enhance your setup. If two or more Beardeds are kept together, provide several basking areas to minimize competition. This will also help to ensure that the dominant, or alpha, male does not unduly harass other individuals.

▶ **A variety of social behaviors can be readily observed in a group of these medium-sized lizards.**

The external ear opening is clearly visible on most lizards

Long claws enable the Bearded Dragon to climb boulders in the wild

As this young adult matures, his beard will darken and may become inflated when he is threatened or when displaying to a potential mate

54

Larger lizards often have a higher metabolic rate and they create large quantities of fecal matter. Soiled areas need regular cleaning and the water should be changed frequently.

Juveniles are normally acquired when they are a couple of months old—usually measuring about 6–7 in (15–17.5 cm). Two Beardeds would require at least a 24 x 12 x 12 in (60 x 30 x 30 cm) vivarium for the first few months of their life. Heating pads are useful to ensure the substrate is dry and warm at all times. Full-spectrum, fluorescent lighting is essential for healthy growth and development—occasional exposure to sunlight is beneficial, but ensure the lizard does not escape its enclosure.

HANDLING

Bearded Dragons tame very quickly while they are still young, especially if coaxed onto your hand with a treat. The claws may feel sharp on a young person's hand, but in general these lizards are very easy to handle. The best way to proceed is to pick up your Bearded gently and place it onto your hand.

FOODS AND FEEDING

Juveniles grow very fast and require a well-supplemented omnivorous diet. Smaller insects, pinkies, and spiders are particularly relished. You can cool your bugs to make them less active and easier for your pet to catch. Chopped fruit and leaves should also be supplied. Juveniles should be fed daily, but be careful not to overfeed. Larger specimens and adults should be fed 4–5 times a week. A bowl of cuttlefish, cut into pieces or grated, allows individuals, especially females, to obtain extra calcium. This is particularly important for healthy egg development in gravid females. Regular vitamin and mineral supplements are required for optimum long term health and development.

When feeding, the social hierarchy, or pecking order, will develop within a group. The largest or dominant lizard will feed first, the others only when it has finished. Similar behavior is seen with basking spots. If the dominant animal moves to a basking area, any underling will move away to avoid confrontation.

BREEDING

A Bearded Dragon becomes sexually mature between its first and second year. Both sexes have spines on the head, neck, and throat, but only the males develop the coal-black throat and tail tip during courtship, or when involved in ritualistic fighting over territory. This will be accompanied by much "head bobbing."

A healthy female may lay six clutches of eggs in a season, averaging 20 eggs per clutch. These are buried deep into the soil—up to 8 in (20 cm)—or into a laying box containing vermiculite. They need to be incubated at 84°F (29°C) for about 60 days. After producing eggs or live young, herptiles benefit from a period of isolation and a nutritional diet in order to recover adequately for future breeding.

▲ **Regular handling of juvenile Beardeds should ensure that they remain tame throughout their life.**

BLUE-TONGUED SKINK

Tiliqua scincoides

True ground dwellers, these snake-like lizards like to scavenge among the tropical leaf litter, brushland, and suburban gardens of their native habitats of north and east Australia and Tasmania.

At least 1000 species of skink have been discovered so far. Most of them are insectivores. They inhabit a wide range of habitats, but are more commonly found in the tropics. In addition to the Blue-tongued Skink, there are a variety of smaller skink species available to the herpetologist. However, only a few are widely available from captive-bred sources. Many may be kept communally alongside other small lizards. Some skinks are native to North America and others are found in Mediterranean Europe. Generally, all skinks have polished scales, flattened and elongated bodies, and possess reduced limbs. Blue-tongued

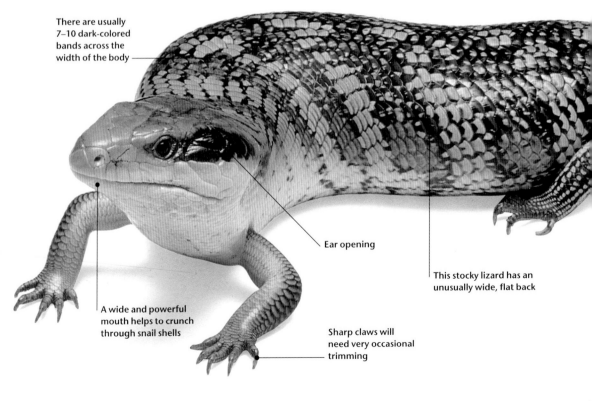

There are usually 7–10 dark-colored bands across the width of the body

Ear opening

This stocky lizard has an unusually wide, flat back

A wide and powerful mouth helps to crunch through snail shells

Sharp claws will need very occasional trimming

skinks, as their name suggests, possess a large blue tongue. The tongue can be flattened and rippled inside an open mouth which, when accompanied by a hiss, acts as a very good deterrent to would-be predators. Although totally defenseless, a bite from an untamed lizard would certainly cause some pain. However, regular handling of your skink will ensure it never feels threatened in captivity and the tongue will be rolled in and out of the mouth as it is stroked on the head or under the chin. Its close relation, the Pink-tongued Skink—which has a bright pink tongue—is not as readily available as the blue-tongued species.

Pink-tongued Skink

Tiliqua gerrardi

The Pink-tongued Skink is also an Australian species and will grow to 18 in (4 cm). Unlike many lizards, the tail of this species is prehensile. Active mainly at night, they enjoy climbing in the lower branches of shrubs in search of snails, slugs, and ripe fruit. They should be cared for in the same way as the blue-tongued variety. Males and females should be housed separately to avoid fighting and only introduced for breeding. They become mature between 2–3 years of age. This species is only sometimes available, and rarely from captive-bred stock.

At birth the live young can be quite large, measuring approximately 6 in (15 cm) in length. Once mature, a fully grown adult can reach a length of 20 in (50 cm). A young Blue-tongued Skink is best purchased at a few months of age, when it is approximately 6–7 in (15–18 cm) long. In captivity, these skinks can live for up to 10 years.

◄ **Highly polished scales, a pointed head, and small legs are all characteristics of the family Scincidae, of which Blue-tongues are one of the larger species.**

CAUTION

Ingested substrate can cause terrible problems for all herptiles. If ingested in sufficient quantities, it can cause serious damage to the stomach and digestive tract. Feed from a dish or bowl where possible to prevent particles sticking to food.

Males usually have a broader-based tail to encompass the twinned reproductive organs that are inside

▲ **This spacious vivarium provides everything a growing Blue-tongued Skink needs.**

CREATING THE RIGHT ENVIRONMENT

A dry, woodland-type habitat with plenty of hiding places and retreats suits these bulky lizards. A vivarium for a single skink or adult pair should measure at least 48 x 12 x 12 in (120 x 30 x 30 cm). Since they actively forage for food, a delicately planted vivarium will be quickly destroyed, so I would suggest you use logs of cork bark and sturdy lumps of wood or rock, securely positioned so that they cannot overturn and injure your pet. Wood chips, peat, and leaf litter will help to create an attractive display within the vivarium.

A maximum daytime temperature range of 77–95°F (25–35°C) would be preferred, with a drop at night to 65–68°F (18–20°C). The combination of a heating pad at one end and a thermostatically controlled spotlight, wired to a timer switch, will warm the tank and create a daytime basking area. The light should be timed to switch off at night, thereby automatically reducing the temperature. A daily spraying is much appreciated and so is a shallow, sturdy bowl of water sunk into the substrate.

Blue-tongues can be housed with other herptiles of a similar size. My own adult skink, Sydney, lives with another Australian lizard species, a Bearded Dragon called Barry.

HANDLING

These lizards thrive in captivity and are usually easy to tame. They can be handled a great deal without obvious signs of distress, although individuals do vary in temperament. Sharp claws may need occasional trimming.

FOODS AND FEEDING

To encourage activity, food should be scattered about, rather than given in a bowl. My skink "Sydney" is fed this way, but the vivarium requires regular cleaning to remove uneaten foodstuffs and soiled areas. For these scavenging omnivores, snails are a favorite food. They will be tracked along their trail, grabbed by the shell and smashed against a log or the side of the vivarium, before the snail itself is swallowed and most of the shell is discarded.

AMAZING FACT

The Pygmy Blue-tongued Skink, a diminutive relation of *Tiliqua scincoides*, was thought for many years to be extinct. Last seen in 1959 in a shed in an Adelaide suburb, this lizard was recently rediscovered, alive and well, close to Adelaide. This lizard only grows to 6 1/2 in (16 cm).

Keeping a Blue-tongued Skink may make you very popular with your gardening neighbors because they will have a handy outlet for all their unwanted pest snails. However, avoid using any snails collected from areas where pesticides may have been used.

Besides snails, these skinks will eat cat or dog food, fruit—they like to lick wet, juicy fruits such as mangoes—some vegetables, and boiled eggs. My own skink is partial to bananas and dog food mash. Richer, processed foods such as cat or dog food should be used sparingly rather than becoming the main diet to reduce the risk of obesity. Crickets and other live foods may hide or out-run these lizards in the vivarium, but cooling the insects in the fridge and then careful hand feeding is an option. Do be careful, however, because a bite from a skink will hurt and may require first aid.

Offer your pet fresh food 3 times a week—uneaten foods, especially meat, should be removed within 24 hours. Garden snails may be collected and maintained in plastic terrariums for use over the winter period.

BREEDING

Although the sexes are not easily distinguished, male skinks usually have a wider head and also a broader-based tail to encompass the twinned reproductive organs that are inside. Mating is initiated by the male biting the female behind the head on the neck area and twisting his body for cloacal contact.

▶ **Although more expensive than other herptiles, these large and impressive lizards, with their bright blue tongues, are easy to maintain.**

If successful, the female will give birth to between 6–25 fully formed young some 4 months later. The exact litter size will depend very much on the size, experience, and health of the mother.

Already large at birth, the babies can be fed a diet similar to that of their parents, but the food should be finely chopped and smaller live foods should be offered. The young may be housed together initially, but they should be separated once fighting and bullying start.

Researching this book has produced some interesting findings. Having worked with, and kept reptiles for many years, I was very surprised to read that breeding records for this species go back at least 100 years, when gas lamps and paraffin heaters were used to heat vivaria. The Reverend Bateman in his book, *The Vivarium*, published in 1897, states that London Zoo and private keepers had breeding success with blue-tongues and that they cost "about 30 shillings when in market."

VEILED CHAMELEON

Chamaeleo calyptratus

The chameleon's amazing ability to change color is much misunderstood. Emotions and territorial posturing, as well as camouflage, are responsible for the rainbow-colored displays.

Chameleons are unlike any other lizard in habitat and appearance. With their unique independently moving eyes and projectile tongue, they will always be a favorite with herpetologists. A few species are now beginning to be bred in captivity for the pet market. Imported specimens rarely survive long, mainly due to the stress of travel and delays at airports and customs. The Veiled Chameleon is now captive bred in large quantities and would appear to be one of the most adaptable species, ideal for the pet keeper willing to invest time and effort.

The Veiled Chameleon, sometimes called the Yemen Chameleon, is native to Saudi Arabia and Yemen. Adult males are usually larger than females and can measure up to 24 in (60 cm), with tail extended. Females usually grow to a maximum of 13 in (33 cm).

Viewed from above, the granulated skin texture and spinal ridge scales can be seen easily

The tail is extremely dextrous and is used as a fifth limb, often to anchor the chameleon while climbing or reaching for prey

▲ **Probably the most incredible lizards on earth, chameleons are a wonder of the natural world.**

With independently moving eyes, the chameleon can judge distance to make an accurate "shot" with its long tongue

The opposing digits on each limb give the chameleon a secure hold on twigs and branches

CREATING THE RIGHT ENVIRONMENT

Larger vivaria suit chameleons best and I would recommend a minimum size of 36 x 36 x 20 in (92 x 92 x 51 cm) to house a single specimen. Veiled Chameleons are very aggressive toward one another, and adults should be housed individually. As bush or shrub dwellers, your chameleon needs a variety of living plants or at least some plastic plants and branches on which it may climb.

One or more spotlights, to create a basking area, will ensure that your pet can warm up properly in the morning before spending the day looking for prey. A temperature of 86°F (30°C) in the basking area, down to 68°F (20°C) in the cooler, shaded part of the vivarium should be available to allow your lizard to thermoregulate with ease. At night the temperature can drop safely to 60°F (15°C). A fluorescent light tube with high UVA/UVB content will ensure good plant and reptile growth.

Chameleons need to drink and eat regularly. Water is preferred in droplet form; indeed, chameleons tend to prefer habitats where heavy dew, or condensation, occurs naturally, since they drink quite a lot in comparison to other reptiles. Mist spray daily and/or provide a pool with water circulating and dripping off branches back into the pool. Good ventilation is essential to the successful, long-term care of these chameleons. A small fan helps to circulate and freshen the air, but it must be placed out of reach of the vivarium inhabitants.

HANDLING

Many Veiled Chameleons tolerate handling relatively well, especially if it involves hand feeding. Start handling your pet while it is still quite young to condition it to this sort of contact on a regular basis. Never pick up the chameleon, as this will cause your pet great offense. Instead, allow it to climb up onto your hand and fingers. If permitted, it will continue to climb until it reaches your shoulders and head.

A M A Z I N G   F A C T

Chameleons are famous for their color-changing ability. They possess pigment-filled cells called chromatophores just beneath the skin's surface. These rapidly expand or contract causing the colors on the skin surface to change. This behavior is triggered by external stimuli, primarily the need for concealment or camouflage. Color fluctuation can be influenced by the lizard's emotional state—angry chameleons will go black. Color changes may also indicate a territorial display, willingness to mate, state of gravidity, and subjugation or low status in a community.

FOODS AND FEEDING

Chameleons enjoy feeding and their method of stalking prey to within range of their long, extendible tongue is fascinating to observe. All live foods can be tried, but flying or climbing species are preferred by these arboreal animals. Variety is the key to providing the range of vitamins and minerals required for healthy development. Some garden-caught food is advised to boost most herptile diets. Larger specimens may accept pinkies, a highly nutritious option.

One method of supplying live foods without the insects dispersing into the vivarium is to attach an opaque plastic terrarium, or similar steep and smooth-sided bowl, to a feeding branch. This will position food within reach of the chameleon and its tongue, without enabling the bugs to reach the branch to escape. Make sure that the bug home is well stocked and that the bugs are well fed—the chameleon will use this "service station" for a fill-up. Try hand feeding by placing a bug in between your extended forefinger and thumb.

Panther Chameleon
Chamaeleo pardalis

Native to Madagascar, Panther Chameleons prefer warm and humid conditions and enjoy climbing on small bushes and shrubs. It is one of the most colorful species of reptile, with males showing the greatest color range—anything from turquoise to fire red and lemon yellow. They are also quite large, with females growing to 13 in (33 cm) and males up to 20 in (51 cm).

Second only to the Veiled Chameleon, these creatures are ideal to keep as vivarium pets. A temperature range of 80–95°F (26.5–35°C) should be supplied and full-spectrum fluorescent lighting is essential for the healthy development of both the chameleon and any housed plants. House males separately because they are very territorial and will fight and injure each other. If a large vivarium is available, you may keep breeding trios together—two females to every male. Unlike the Veiled species, Panthers are insectivorous, eating almost any of the commonly available live foods and the odd pinky or small lizard (vertebrate food should not be fed live to your pet).

Unusually, the Veiled Chameleon is an omnivorous creature and will accept a wide range of leaves, fruit, and vegetables—these should be dusted with vitamin and mineral supplements.

BREEDING

Veiled Chameleons are sexually dimorphic, that is, the sexes differ in apprearance. Males have a larger casque (a helmet-like structure on their heads), small "spurs" on their back legs, and are generally bigger than females.

They are prolific breeders and egg layers, and a female may lay clutches numbering between 25–80 eggs, 3–4 times a year. The clutch size as with most animals, is dependent on the size, age, experience, and health of the mature female. This productivity does take its toll eventually and females rarely survive much beyond their fifth clutch. The eggs are buried in soil or sand and should be placed in vermiculite and incubated at 80–85°F (27–29.5°C) during the day, with a slight drop at night to 75°F (24°C).

Other aspects of chameleon husbandry are too complex to go into at length, but put very simply, Veiled Chameleons should be kept separately and only introduced for mating. Only juveniles should be housed together, and then only for a few months, since they reach sexual maturity between 4–6 months of age. Young females can be mated from about 5 months of age.

Juvenile chameleons, like most herptiles, grow rapidly and it is in these first crucial months that the most varied and well-supplemented diet will enable them to grow up into healthy, mature specimens. They need a larger range and variety of insect prey than the adults, which tend to enjoy a more omnivorous diet.

Drosophila and other winged prey are particularly relished by juveniles, who can devour very large quantities at this tender age. Wild-caught insects help to ensure a beneficial supply of nutrients.

▲ Of all the species of chameleon available in captivity, the Veiled Chameleon is taking the herpetological world by storm. It is a breedable, attractive, and interesting species to keep, which thrives as a pet under the right conditions.

UROMASTYX

Uromastyx acanthinurus

Also known as Dabb Lizards, these unusual looking creatures are found in the southern Mediterranean and in the Middle East. They spend much of their time scrambling over rock piles and dunes.

Growing to 18 in (45 cm) in length, this is a large, heavy-bodied lizard with a head not unlike a tortoise. Because of its size, I would recommend that only a novice with enough time and space should keep this species. Their color develops as juveniles and can be anything from yellowish to red in tone with a dark brown base coloration. These lizards tend to live for 7–10 years, but 15 years is a possibility.

CREATING THE RIGHT ENVIRONMENT

For a single adult a vivarium measuring 48 x 20 x 20 in (120 x 50 x 50 cm) is ideal, furnished with rocks, washed sand, and desert-style decor. Full spectrum fluorescent lights and a safely positioned and protected ceramic heater are both necessary to ensure full maturing and successful breeding of these lizards. The hot end of the vivarium should be heated with a powerful 60 watt or 100 watt infra-red lamp controlled by a thermostat so your pet can bask at temperatures around 95°F (35°C). Another part of the vivarium must be considerably cooler, 68–72°F (20–22°C), so they can thermoregulate as required.

Their native desert environment is very hot and to escape excess heat they will retreat into cool burrows. Drainpipes or artificial rock hides are suitable for providing retreats. Cork bark is ideal because it is light and can be pegged or siliconed into a range of structures. Ensure your rocks or shelters cannot collapse and injure your pet.

Your Uromastyx should be mist-sprayed at least twice weekly. Once every four weeks give them a bath in clean, tepid, shallow water to allow them to re-hydrate if required, and to aid the periodic process of shedding.

HANDLING

A mature, wild-caught specimen is capable of giving a bad bite but, in general, this species seems to be of a pleasant character. If acquired as a captive-bred juvenile, they will tame easily and quickly. Encourage your pet to come to you for food. Move slowly and deliberately so that it is not startled into running away. Eventually it should sit on your hand—at least for a while! Like other medium-sized lizards, you can pick them up gently with one or two hands.

AMAZING FACT

These lizards wedge themselves into crevices to make it very difficult for a predator to extract them. When they are too cold and without the energy to flee they are likely to use their club-like tails as a weapon. The vigorous blows can wound any would-be predator, even venomous Horned Vipers.

FOODS AND FEEDING

Virtually herbivorous, their diet should consist of mainly green leaf foods with pieces of vegetable and fruit added. Carrots, peas, beans, and hibiscus leaves are also enjoyed. Some insect foods may be accepted. Feed every other day and remove uneaten foods on the second day to minimize fouling. Supply food on shallow trays away from the main basking spot to avoid desiccation of the food.

This species is likely to aestivate, at least for short periods. It would appear that this correlates to its behavior in the wild and you should not worry unduly if your Uromastyx rests without eating for 1–2 weeks in one of its favorite retreats.

BREEDING

Trying to breed Uromastyx is difficult but not impossible. Mating occurs in the spring and eggs are laid in May or June. Eggs should be incubated in a dryish medium of vermiculite or perlite at 86–89°F (30–33°C) for approximately 12 weeks. When breeding any herptile, try to ensure that the adults are given a very nutritious and calcium-rich diet to prepare them for the physically exhausting process of producing and laying eggs.

Uromastyx are quite aggressive to each other and are best kept singularly or in trios—one male to two females—but only if very large accommodation is available. After mating, the female should be housed on her own with a suitable amount of substrate to encourage egg laying.

Inhabiting a harsh, arid environment, they need an occasional bath or spray of water—it will darken the skin, the body swelling visibly as water is absorbed

A small and plump captive-bred juvenile is the ultimate choice because it will readily adapt to life in the vivarium

The armored spiky scales on the tail create a formidable weapon

▶ Only the healthiest specimens should be considered for a pet. Avoid any thin, inactive individuals and watch out for damaged or swollen digits, a thin bony tail, and a dirty vent.

GIANT GREEN IGUANA

Iguana iguana

These "tree chickens," as the West Indians call them, spend their time grazing on leaves, fruits and flowers in lush tropical vegetation. Good swimmers, they will dive into water to avoid predators.

Native to Central and South America, the Giant Green Iguana is probably the most commonly kept large lizard but it is only suitable for those hobbyists with considerable space and time available to them. Not only are they large, they can live for 10–15 years in captivity. Although basically green, Giant Green Iguanas can display a range of colors. My iguana (pictured right) has a remarkably blue head and a colorful dewlap, or throat pouch.

When buying an iguana it is important to get one as young as possible because early handling will help to foster a good relationship between you. Look for a lizard that is not too bony at the tail base, is alert and not sluggish, and preferably one that looks interested or will come towards you when food is offered. Distressed or scared individuals will shoot off in flight at the first sign of trouble.The temperament of lizards vary and you must hope to choose one that will become used to, and enjoy, your company rather than attempt to bite or flee.

CREATING THE RIGHT ENVIRONMENT

Iguanas need more space as they grow, with height being the most important factor to consider, although they will use the ground area too. Start off with, at the very minimum, a 36 x 18 x 12 in (92 x 38 x 30 cm) vivarium for your baby iguana. Adult iguanas require a custom-made vivarium measuring a minimum 48 x 72 x 48 in (120 x 180 x 120 cm).

Provide sturdy branches, plastic plants for shade, and a large, non-spillable water dish. Cork logs make ideal retreats and your iguana will probably sleep in one, especially if it is nice and warm. A good hot basking spot, 86°F (30°C) is required for this diurnal reptile. A full spectrum fluorescent light is also essential for maintaining your lizard's long-term health.

▲ **As it grows, this hatchling iguana will require considerable space to allow for its healthy development.**

▼ These truly magnificent creatures are suitable only for those hobbyists with the considerable space and time to tame and care for them adequately.

▲ The long, sharp claws and the elongated toes enable iguanas to climb into the rain-forest canopy.

HANDLING

Iguanas are not easy to handle unless they are very tame. Claws grow long and lacerate human flesh, so you should trim them occasionally, taking care to avoid the "quick," or living part of the claw. Very tame iguanas may be walked on a leash or perched on a shoulder, but most never tame to this extent.

Less tame individuals need professional restraining—using long leather gauntlets to protect yourself is recommended. The iguana should be held firmly behind the neck and above the rear legs and the tail should be tucked under your arm to avoid its painful whip. Juveniles are likely to drop their tails for defensive reasons but this ability is lost once iguanas mature.

FOODS AND FEEDING

Adult iguanas are herbivorous and will eat a wide variety, and quantity, of foods. It is important not to overfeed your pet on richer, "preferred" foods since, in the wild, the bulk of its diet is made up of poor quality foods. Adult iguanas should be fed every other day or so. A large stainless steel bowl filled with a mixture of fruits, leaves, and vegetables is sufficient. Depending on the season, you could include the following: chopped

AMAZING FACT

In the Caribbean, iguanas are called tree chickens, and an adult, once cooked, can feed a family of fou romaine, corn, cucumber, flowers, dandelion, cooked potato, apple, pear, kiwi fruit, banana (including skin), grapes, green beans, kale, broccoli, melon, plums, and mango. Remove the food bowl on the second day and replace with more food, at the latest, on the third day.

Juvenile iguanas will eat much the same thing, but in a smaller, finely chopped form and adding some live foods—crickets, grasshoppers, and waxworms—is necessary. Taming and feeding your juvenile goes hand in hand. You really must invest considerable time in taming your iguana so that you can both enjoy a good relationship.

BREEDING

During copulation, a male iguana will firmly bite and hold the female at the neck or head. By twisting his body partially under hers, mating is possible and can last from a minute to nearly half an hour. A gestation period of 50–90 days is typical, and the female will dig a long chamber about 20 in (50 cm) deep and $39^{1}/_{2}$–79 in (1–2 m) in

length. Up to 40 eggs are deposited over several hours and, after burying them, they are left to incubate in the warm soil. Under optimum conditions they hatch about 10–15 weeks later and the youngsters spend the first months of life chasing invertebrates and feeding on leaves and flowers.

Iguanas are raised in Central America and bred in zoos and institutions in the USA and other countries. Captive breeding is only likely in very large enclosures. It is unlikely for most pets and, indeed, as they grow too large for their vivaria, many are disposed of or end up in the local zoo or wildlife park. Home breeding is not recommended.

C A U T I O N

Many pet stores sell the small emerald green juveniles that only measure 10 in (25 cm). Bear in mind, however, that they will eventually grow into a formidable 79-in (2-m) long adult with a strong tail that will lash at anything or anyone threatening it.

◀ An enlarged scale, clearly visible beneath the ear opening, may serve as a false eye. When coupled with jagged spines along the length of its back and on the edge of its extendable dewlap, an iguana can make itself look quite formidable.

MEDITERRANEAN SPUR-THIGHED TORTOISE

Testudo graeca

These hardy creatures are native to the Mediterranean and may be found in Spain, Greece, and Turkey. They are quite well suited to temperate climates but do require a little help to grow, thrive, and breed.

Thousands of Mediterranean Spur-thighed Tortoises are bred every year in captivity. A captive-bred baby measuring 3 in (7.5 cm) is an ideal acquisition. Initially, it will need to be kept in a vivarium indoors in winter, and kept in an outside enclosure during the summer. The shell color can vary from yellow to black and they obtain a length of about 8 in.

CREATING THE RIGHT ENVIRONMENT

For all but the youngest juveniles, who need to be penned, tortoises may be kept in a walled or fenced garden for much of the spring and summer months when the garden is frost free. A hutch provides shelter from rain and excesses of temperatures. It should be fitted with a heat source or infra-red lamp to keep chills at bay and to enable

The strong claws enable tortoises to dig burrows for hibernation or egg laying

The upper part of the shell, the carapace, and the lower portion, the plastron, are joined together by a narrow strip of shell between the front and rear legs

▲ **A youthful 15 year old, this female tortoise is of prime breeding age. You should expect at least 30–50 years from a captive-bred animal.**

Tortoises have a strong horny beak that can cut and tear the tough vegetation upon which they feed

HIBERNATION

Tortoises from temperate climates should hibernate during early to late autumn. People have found that tortoises hibernate naturally outdoors, where they dig themselves into a sheltered spot, often under a tree. Depending on their choice of resting place, and the winter weather, they may do well but are exposed to all sorts of risks. These include severe weather, damp conditions, and being dug up by predators. It is much better to hibernate your tortoise in a cold (unheated) but frost-free cellar or garden shed.

Tortoises must empty their digestive tract before hibernating. A gradual reduction in temperature a few weeks prior to hibernation should work because the tortoise's appetite declines but it still digests food in the system. An underweight tortoise should not be hibernated and if in doubt, visit your vet or specialist pet store for advice. I hibernate mine in a hutch furnished with straw (avoid hay because cut grass can cause lung problems) from around September/October to March, depending on the severity of the seasons. Hibernated tortoises should be checked on a regular basis. Upon waking, a warm bath helps them to rehydrate and clears the eyes, nostrils, and mouth of any debris and usually stimulates a bowel movement prior to a feeding. It is not advisable to hibernate baby tortoises until they have a plastron length of around 5 in (13 cm).

the tortoise to be active on cooler days. (Make sure the electrical circuitry is installed by a professional). Locate the hutch in a sheltered spot, away from direct wind and sunlight. Ensure that ponds and other deep water features are fenced off to prevent your tortoise from drowning.

Despite their reputation, a healthy tortoise is a fast creature, which will crash through flowerbeds to smell plants before trying them. They can be deterred from doing so by placing 10-in (25-cm) high boards around the garden. In the morning, they like to orientate themselves toward the sun, and a south-facing slope is appreciated to help catch those all-important rays. They soon learn the location of their hutches, the best sunbathing spots and favorite places to rest, feed, or sleep.

▶ This 2-year-old Californian-bred Mediterranean Spur-thighed Tortoise is being held carefully using two hands.

HANDLING

Tortoises tame quickly, especially when offered tasty tidbits. The tendency for the head to be withdrawn gradually decreases as they become used to human company. Tortoises can be held firmly from either side, with thumbs on top of the shell and fingers underneath the body—this is the usual method.

FOODS AND FEEDING

The Mediterranean Spur-thighed Tortoise is an herbivore and will be satisfied entirely with most fruit and vegetable matter you offer. Vitamin supplements should be added to the food to promote healthy shell formation, although ability to graze in a garden and exposure to sunlight will usually fulfill most vitamin and mineral requirements.

My own tortoises are offered chopped fruit and vegetables on roofing slates (flat and easy to clean) placed in the garden. Consider offering the following, making sure you provide a good selection: Brussels sprouts, chickweed, clover, runner beans, bok choy, grated carrot, cress, peas, broccoli, bindweed, romaine lettuce, cauliflower, rose petals, cucumber, and soft fruits (not citrus). They can also forage—I positively encourage dandelions, a favorite tortoise food, but not every gardener's favorite weed.

Food preferences will vary, but experience will help to guide you. Iceberg lettuce should only be a small percentage of your tortoise's diet, no matter how much your pet enjoys it, since it is of low nutritional value. Although normally herbivorous, some tortoises seem to enjoy a small amount of meat in their diet. In the wild tortoises will eat available carrion, such as dead birds and snakes. Be careful not to overfeed on meat and restrict it to 1–5% of their total diet.

Since tortoises come from the world's naturally arid environments, much of the moisture they require actually comes from the foods they

▼ **Providing a variety of foods helps to ensure that your pet tortoise will grow and develop into a healthy adult.**

consume. Since your pets are confined to a relatively small area, compared to their native range, they cannot seek out supplemental sources of moisture. You must also provide your pet clean water in a shallow dish.

BREEDING

Adult male and female tortoises are easily distinguished. The female has a shorter tail and a flat underside, while the male has a longer tail and a concave underside that enables him to mount the female for mating.

▲ This large "pet home" unit is ideal for rearing baby tortoises, keeping them warm and well fed.

The best male/female ratio for breeding tortoises is one male to three or four females. Males dominate their females. By ramming his shell against hers, biting her legs or tail, the male will force her to give up trying to escape his advances and enable mating to take place. Mating is unmistakable, with the sound of much clanking and bashing of shells prior to the male vocalizing once mating is underway. The rough courtship of the male can cause considerable distress and some injury to the female, whose legs may become sore and bloody as a result of his continual advances— hence the recommendation for a harem of three or four females to divide the male's attention among them.

Eggs are buried about 6 in (15 cm) deep in the soil and so well covered by the female that, unless egg laying is actually witnessed, it may be impossible to locate the site. Eggs must be removed, without turning, and placed in vermiculite at between 82–90°F (28–32°C) at a

relative humidity of 70%. Hopefully, these will then hatch approximately 75–85 days later.

For their first year of life, keep baby tortoises in an indoor vivarium under full-spectrum lights at 77–82°F (25–28°C). Move them to small, contained runs in the garden during the warmest months, where access to real ultraviolet rays will help with healthy shell formation. At this stage they are still vulnerable, so be aware of possible predators.

AMAZING FACT

Tortoises helped Darwin to develop the revolutionary idea of evolution. He noticed that, although very similar in appearance to those on the South American mainland, the tortoises on the Galapagos Islands were much larger. He worked out that over millions of years small changes take place in each new generation due to the different environmental conditions faced by a species. These offshore tortoises had gradually developed into giants.

Reptiles 2

Snakes

These predators belong to the largest order of reptiles—the Squamata. Secretive by nature and often solitary, they spend much of their lives concealed in hollow logs or mammal burrows. Some of the more commonly kept species include Milk Snakes, Ball Pythons, and Garter Snakes.

All snakes are predatory vertebrates. They are found throughout the warmer parts of the world and they thrive in numerous habitats, including open sea, deserts, underground, or high up in tree canopies.

Snakes, like lizards, chelonia, and amphibians, are ectothermic. This means that they rely on their environment to satisfy their heat requirements. In extreme temperature conditions, many temperate species hibernate in winter and tropical species aestivate in summer. Some species of Garter Snake are only active for three months of the year because their natural environment is extremely cold.

Snakes have evolved from, and can be described as, specially modified lizards that have adapted to a limbless existence. Their scales may be flat, overlapping, or keeled with a raised ridge in the center to allow them to grip

surfaces successfully. Periodic shedding replaces the old skin. In snakes the old skin is always discarded and is not consumed as it is by most amphibians and many lizards.

The structure of the skeleton varies from species to species. It is more elongated in snakes than in any other reptile and consists of up to 400 separate vertebrae, mostly attached to long curved ribs. The backbone is extremely flexible when moved from side to side, but has little vertical movement.

Snakes move by contracting and expanding the body lengthwise while simultaneously gripping the ground by pressing the body and ribs onto large wide ventral scales. Other methods of movement employed by snakes include side winding and a concertina style of movement. Some primitive snakes still display visible remnants of legs possessed by their lizard ancestors.

▲ Typically for reptiles, the bones of snakes do not stop growing once they mature and continue to grow throughout their lives.

▶ Snakes are seen by many people as beautiful and fascinating creatures that should be encouraged as household pets. Colorful species, such as this Corn Snake, are bred to the extent that they may soon be described as domesticated animals.

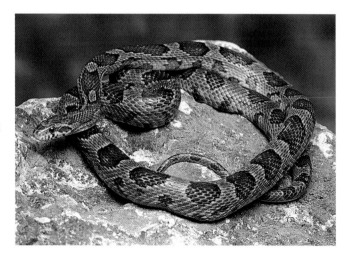

The upper and lower jaws are loosely connected to the skull and may be expanded greatly—most species eat prey much larger than their head/neck size would suggest. All snakes are carnivores and conume food whole. Food is either swallowed alive constricted within coils and asphyxiated, or killed by an injection of lethal venom. Snakes are unable to chew or cut food into portions and prey is simply swallowed in one piece, usually head first.

As predatory reptiles, a snake's success as a hunter is dependant on the combined use of the eyes and tongue. Snakes cannot open or close their eyes; in effect, the eyelid is shut but transparent. A snake's visual perception is very different from our own. We can see individual objects, whereas snakes can only see or perceive an object when it moves or changes in some way. The tongue collects tiny airborne particles that are analyzed by a special structure called the Jacobson's organ in the roof of the mouth. A snake's tongue is forked and it effectively tastes or smells the air in "stereo," each fork providing some sense of direction.

Snakes have no visible ear openings and do not hear sounds in the way that humans can. They are sensitive to ground vibrations, which are felt through the lower jaw.

The tail of a male snake is often longer than that of a female. It is also generally wider at the base where the twinned or hemi-penis is enclosed. Females lay a leathery shelled egg. Some species, mainly those from temperate areas, incubate their eggs internally and give birth to fully formed young. Snakes rarely provide parental care—the majority of eggs are simply laid, buried, and abandoned. A few species, however, such as some cobras and pythons, do guard and protect their nests.

▶ As reptiles grow, they will periodically shed their skin. This process normally starts around the head. A juvenile snake may shed its skin every month, but an adult will do so only 3–4 times a year.

KING SNAKES
Lampropeltis getulus

King Snakes are a wide-ranging species found from Canada in the north to Ecuador in the south. They are very popular pets due to their size, great color, and variable patterns.

All King Snakes are ophiophagous. Normally, they will feed on other snakes in the wild, but are generalized carnivores in captivity. They feed well and will eat almost any prey—birds, lizards, frogs, and rodents. They are so popular that many thousands are bred by hobbyists and professional herpetologists every year for the pet trade.

The common subspecies grow to about 48 in (120 cm) and live for 10–15 years. Subspecies to look out for include the following:

Californian King Snake   *Lampropeltis getulus californiae*

Florida King Snake   *Lampropeltis getulus floridana*

Mexican Black King Snake   *Lampropeltis getulus nigritus*

CREATING THE RIGHT ENVIRONMENT
House King Snakes separately because they are cannibalistic. A clean, dry vivarium heated to 80–90°F (26.5–32°C) at the warmest end and 75°F (24°C) at the cooler end would be ideal. These snakes rarely climb so the height of your vivarium is far less important than the provision of hides in both the warm and cool parts of the unit. A vivarium measuring 36 x 12 x 12 in (90 x 30 x 30 cm) is more than adequate. There are no supplementary lighting requirements, since background daylight is sufficient.

Paper or wood chips are the most commonly used substrates. The use of rocks, cork bark, and a panoramic background can help to create an attractive display. These snakes do climb to a small extent, but branches are not essential. Fresh water should be available in a shallow water dish, large enough for the occasional bath.

▲ The temperature is controlled by a thermostat and the artificial plants provide a cool retreat that can be regularly mist sprayed.

HANDLING

The very youngest King Snakes will vibrate their tails angrily, strike at you, attempt to wriggle away, or defecate on you when handled because they think you are a hungry predator. The best course of action is to continue to handle your juvenile a few times a week. Eventually, it will realize that you are not a threat, but a friend offering occasional food rewards.

Most King Snakes tame very well and rarely offend their keeper by biting. Most hobbyists, however, will be bitten by accident sooner or later and, apart from the initial shock, your snake is unlikely to cause much damage.

A King Snake will happily coil around your hands and wrists as it explores. Remember not to handle your snake after feeding or before a shed.

Rather than waiting in ambush, King Snakes actively hunt using sight and smell to locate prey

▶ King Snakes are a highly variable species—some are striped and the darker markings can range from jet black to a chocolate color. The white markings are also variable, ranging from a creamy yellow to pure white.

King Snakes are secretive and spend much of their time hidden from view

The clear scale covering the eye turns a bluish color when the snake is about to shed

The forked tongue collects tiny airborne particles that are analyzed by a structure on the roof of the mouth

79

FOODS AND FEEDING

King Snakes will happily eat each other and any other herptile within reach and, therefore, need to be kept singly. Providing you have purchased a healthy captive-bred specimen you should have no feeding problems. They are most likely to refuse food just before shedding and will be at their hungriest just after. For a more nervous specimen, leave food in a hide box to make them feel more secure.

A diet of dead rodents is sufficient for all the snake's nutritional needs, assuming it is eating healthy well-fed rodents. Even juvenile snakes will usually accept young mice or pinkies. Many keepers and breeders will also provide their snakes with small lizards, such as *Anolis* sp. and *Sceloporus*, to encourage feeding and to offer some variety in the diet. You may not be able to do this. Because mice are easily obtained ready frozen, needing only to be thawed and warmed, they provide the bulk of most pet King Snakes' diets. Supply food in a size relative to your pet; the bulge created upon swallowing food should never be abnormally large. Feed your snake as much as it will eat in 15–20 minutes, every 6–8 days.

PREDATOR & PREY

King Snakes eat a variety of foods in the wild—other snakes, lizards, birds, and even reptile eggs. They are marauding hunters, actively seeking prey above ground and below in mammal burrows and tunnels. They possess the unusual ability to kill more than one prey at a time. The first victim is seized in the jaws, and subsequent prey is pushed against a rock or smothered in coils. In turn, King Snakes are preyed upon by raptors and mammals, such as the coyote, as well as other King Snakes.

BREEDING

These snakes are most likely to mate after a period of hibernation. They should be kept for several weeks, without feeding, at temperatures of 55–60°F (12.5–15°C). After this period, raise the temperature to their normal vivarium conditions. When ready for mating, usually after a shed, the female releases hormones to attract the male. Mating snakes should be watched to ensure one does not eat the other.

Return the female to her vivarium. Insert a laying container filled with dampened sphagnum moss for the female to lay her eggs. About 5–7 weeks after mating 5–17 eggs will be laid, each measuring up to 2 1/2 in (5 cm) in length and 3/4 in (2 cm) in width. These should be removed and incubated in vermiculite at 75°F (24°C).

Within 70 days the eggs will hatch into 9 1/2 in- (25-cm) long babies. Once shedding has taken place, usually 12–16 days after birth, they will be ready to feed on the smallest of pinkies. At 4–6 months of age they are an ideal purchase as a pet. This species matures at 2 1/2–3 years.

AMAZING FACT

King Snakes are noted for their unusual ability to kill and consume venomous snakes such as Coral Snakes and Pit Vipers. Although they show little or no ill effects from the bites of American Pit Vipers, immunity to the venom would seem to be variable within the species.

▲ This chocolate and banana colored specimen is another variation of the Californian King Snake.

▶ The glossy Mexican Black King Snake is a very popular choice for the vivarium.

▼ Florida King Snakes are one of the heavier, more solidly built species.

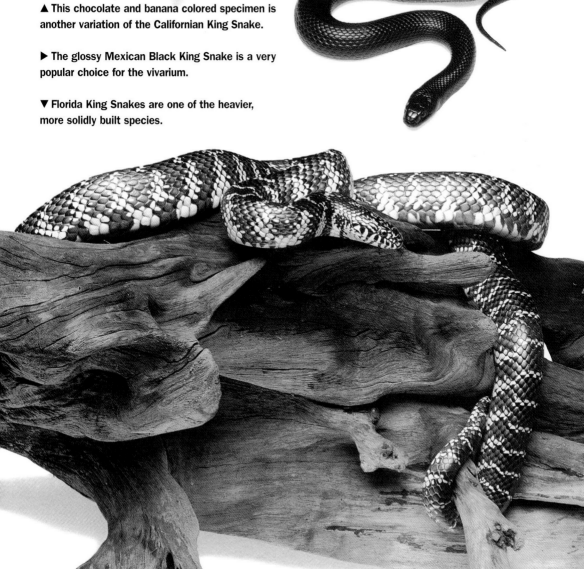

MILK SNAKES

Lampropeltis triangulum

Noted for their eye-catching bands of color, they are also the smallest members of the King Snake family. Possessing cannibalistic tendencies, they need to be housed individually.

This American species is found in an area ranging from southern Canada to northern South America. They live in a variety of habitats, ranging from swamps to deserts.

There are about 25 recognized varieties, or subspecies, of Milk Snakes and they are the smaller and more colorful members of a group of snakes called King Snakes. In Latin their name, *Lampropeltis*, means "shiny shield." Milk Snakes are well known for their habits of eating venomous American snakes and are best kept separately to avoid unfortunate accidents.

Depending on the subspecies, these snakes will grow to 20–48 in (50–120 cm) in length and will live for approximately 10–15 years.

Milk Snakes are widely available in pet shops and directly from breeders. Look out for those listed below, since they are available from captive-bred stocks and are easy to maintain in captivity.

Pueblan Milk Snake   *Lampropeltis triangulum campbelli*

Mexican Milk Snake   *Lampropeltis triangulum annulata*

Honduran Milk Snake   *Lampropeltis triangulum hondurensis*

CREATING THE RIGHT ENVIRONMENT

Milk Snakes should be housed individually because they have cannibalistic tendencies. They prefer small, secure, accommodation and, since they are unlikely to climb much, your vivarium does not have to be very tall either.

They spend much of their time hiding below ground and, given the choice, your pet is likely to wriggle under the substrate and spend many hours resting. A mixture of wood chips, sand and dried moss is suitable. Add dried pine cones, driftwood, cleaned leaves and cacti skeleton to enhance the appearance of your pet's home.

▲ **This glass vivarium provides a secure and desirable home for a Milk Snake. It has retreats and is warmed from below by an undertank heater.**

A 24 x 12 x 12 in (60 x 30 x 30 cm) vivarium is ideal for a 20–24 in (50–60 cm) specimen. Establish a temperature gradient, keeping the hottest parts at about 86°F (30°C) and the cooler areas at 70–74°F (21–23°C). Under vivarium heating will warm the substrate—using undertank heaters is the most suitable method. Wire them to a thermostat and ensure they cover no more than half of the ground area. No extra lighting is required.

HANDLING

Most pet Milk Snakes become tame and easy to handle without problems developing. However, some may want to be left alone and they will defecate, writhe about, or may regurgitate food if handling is attempted too soon after a feed. Select a relatively tame snake to start with and then patience, persistence, and common sense will help you to tame your pet within a short amount of time.

FOODS AND FEEDING

Always feed these snakes separately to avoid one snake mistaking his fellow house mate for a meal. Never keep adults and young snakes together because the adults are likely to eat their younger friends.

Your recently acquired Milk Snake should be settled into a diet of pinkies and, so long as it feeds well, it will grow quite rapidly. Baby snakes will usually begin to feed after their first slough at 10–14 days. They should then be offered 2–3 small pinkies at a sitting, every 5–6 days. At several months of age (when they are best purchased as pets) they can be offered several pinkies or furries—as much as they will consume in about 10 minutes—every 7–10 days.

Feed your adult snake as much as can be eaten in 10–15 minutes, every 6–8 days. The food a snake consumes should leave a visible, but not abnormal-sized, swelling along its body. You may find that after feeding regularly for several weeks your pet may refuse food for a number of weeks. Do not worry, it is simply full and this is quite normal.

BREEDING

These snakes are not sexually dimorphic, so there is no easy way to sex them. Most snakes will be sexed by the breeder or dealer who is supplying the specimen. For breeding information see the section on King Snakes on p. 80.

Some Milk and King Snakes are known as tri-colors

▲ A Pueblan Milk Snake, *Lampropeltis triangulum campbelli*, displaying a bold three-colored pattern.

Large scales on the head have given the Milk Snake its Latin name— *Lampropeltis,* meaning shiny shield

CORN SNAKES

Elaphe guttata guttata

This colorful species, also known as the Red Rat Snake, is one of the most commonly kept and bred snakes. They are easy to keep, making them an ideal introduction to snake keeping.

There is much to recommend Corn Snakes for the first time keeper. They feed well, are usually of good temperament and are very attractive. Now available in a number of color variations, they have popular names such as Snow and King Corn. Adults, measuring 31 1/2–60 in (80–150 cm) can live up to 20 years, although 10 to 15 years is more common.

CREATING THE RIGHT ENVIRONMENT

They require a dry setup with temperatures between 77–86°F (25–30°C) in summer, down to 66°F (20°C) in winter. An adult pair requires at least a 36 x 24 x 24 in (90 x 60 x 60 cm) vivarium. Juveniles should be housed in smaller plastic rearing boxes measuring 9 1/2 x 4 x 4 in (24 x 10 x 10 cm) or in a 24 x 12 x 12 in (60 x 30 x 30 cm) vivarium.

The red markings provide surprisingly effective camouflage in their natural environment

Corn Snakes are excellent climbers

Snakes cannot blink—the eyelid is permanently closed but transparent

▲ **Attractive colorations and good temperament have endeared these snakes to many pet keepers.**

▲ Corn Snakes require access to fresh water for drinking and thoroughly enjoy the occasional bath. Increased humidity helps snakes shed without difficulty.

FOODS AND FEEDING

Corn Snakes feed well and can be given the domestic mouse, *Mus musculus*, for all of their natural life. However, you should be aware that newly hatched Corn Snakes, typically measuring only 9–14 in (23–36 cm), can have a bit of trouble getting started. Even pinkies can be too large or difficult for them to swallow at this age. In the wild some baby Corns feed on baby frogs or lizards until they grow to a size when rodents can be easily consumed.

A number of substrates are suitable, ranging from plain paper to bark chips and wood chips. Reptile grass is a useful and more aesthetically pleasing alternative to newspaper. A branch for climbing and 1–2 hides must be provided. Make sure a shallow water dish, large enough for the occasional bath, is available. Leaves may be added to make the cage more decorative—freeze these before use to kill potential pests, such as mites or ticks.

If your baby Corn is not feeding, offer mouse legs or a warmed up sliced pinky—not a pleasant job, but satisfying when your snake does start to feed. After a couple of sheds, your pet should be able to eat pinkies thawed in warm water and blotted dry. A snake on this sort of diet is known as a defrost feeder. I would advise buying a Corn Snake when it is a minimum of six months of age. By this stage it should be a good, regular feeder, well past its problem age.

HANDLING

Baby snakes are usually very defensive to begin with and will hiss and strike out at anything that moves. Once you have one in your hand it should start to calm down; the snake will gradually realize that the scent of a human hand causes them no harm. When picking up an adult snake, support it along the length of the body. You should not dangle a snake by its neck or tail.

▶ Juveniles need regular handling to condition them to human contact. This specimen is learning that contact will not harm it.

Feed hatchlings on very small pinkies every few days. Juveniles will require several pinkies or furries every 7–10 days and adults will require 2–3 adult mice every 2 weeks.

Grown mice should provide all the necessary vitamins and minerals for healthy growth and development. Make sure you only feed domestic mice and avoid using any wild-caught prey. Although your snake will quite happily eat any animal that your cat kills, any animal caught in this way may introduce internal parasites, such as worms.

Corn Snakes kill their prey by constriction. Their usual method is to strike out and bite the prey on the head. The snake then coils around its victim and squeezes, thus asphyxiating the prey. For ease of consumption, the prey is almost always swallowed head first. Even when feeding on pre-killed rodents, many pet snakes will still go through the motions of "killing." Once they are satisfied that the prey is ready to consume, they will usually smell it from end to end and, by expanding their jaws, they can consume food larger than their head/neck size would otherwise indicate.

BREEDING

Most male snakes have longer tails than the females. Measure similarly aged snakes from the vent to the tail tip to ascertain the correct sex of your snake.

Breeding usually takes place during spring and mating is characterized by an intertwined embrace. Mating in snakes provides an ideal opportunity to watch an ancient but effective reproductive process. A keen male will follow

▲ **Babies are initially reared in small containers to give them a sense of security. Water, shelter, warmth, and food are essential for health.**

a prospective female around the vivarium often biting her and rubbing against the length of her body. Eventually, he will bite her firmly on the neck and pull the weight of his body on top of hers. He will stimulate her by rubbing and making wave-like motions against her cloacal region and mating will take place. Courtship and mating can last for several hours.

Up to 20 eggs are laid in a well-concealed spot in the soil—suitable places are under a dish or a log, or within a hide box. Incubate them in dampened vermiculite at 82–86°F (28–30°C). The eggs will then hatch after approximately 10 weeks. Corn Snakes mature at 2–3 years, when they are about $31\frac{1}{2}$ in (80 cm) long, and can breed until they are about 10 years of age.

VARIETIES

The following varieties of Corn Snake are available from captive-bred stocks.

Amelanistic Corn (albino)	Lacking black pigment in skin and eye, they display a red and orange pattern.
Motley Corn	Pale orange in color, they possess an unusual and irregular pattern.
Black Corn	These snakes display a predominance of black pigmentation and are often completely black.

Color variations found in some Corn Snakes are the direct result of the inbreeding of naturally occurring, but rare, genetic mutations. However, inbreeding does carry the risk of lower fertility and other health problems. A normal Corn Snake is, I think, the nicest and best snake to keep, but many people prefer snakes that display unusual skin colorations.

In the wild, many of these unusually colored snakes would be marked out as easy prey and, as a result, would be much less likely to survive for very long. They are abundant only under captive conditions where such unusual markings are deemed desirable. Within any population of animals such mutations will appear occasionally.

▲ This juvenile Amelanistic Corn Snake has no black pigment in the skin and the eyes are usually pink or red. They are more sensitive to light and are generally of a more delicate disposition than those with normal coloration.

▶ This young Black Corn has black saddles instead of the natural red coloration. Breeders now produce a range of color variations.

HOUSE SNAKES

Lamprophis fuliginosus

These chocolate brown snakes are a common African species and are frequently found in, under, or near houses in villages and towns. In the wild, they feed on rodents and lizards.

This is a relatively new species to be bred and available in the herpetological trade. Although not as commonly available as the more colorful King and Corn Snakes, they are, however, easy to keep and breed. This snake is highly recommended for the novice snake keeper because they are rated as one of the easiest to handle. House Snakes can grow up to 44 in (112 cm) and will live for 10–15 years.

▼ **At 12 in (30 cm), this juvenile is ready to go to a new home. Eager to feed and easy to breed it is an ideal first choice for the novice keeper.**

Smooth scales may feel moisturized but never slimy

The milk chocolate color of body and head contrasts strongly with the creamy belly scales

CREATING THE RIGHT ENVIRONMENT

These snakes are best kept in a dry, woodland-style setup. The floor should be furnished with a substrate, such as bark chips. Logs, cork bark or other suitable hiding places also need to be provided. They love their hiding places; six of my young house snakes, each measuring 12 in (30 cm), share a 24 x 8 x 8 in (60 x 20 x 20 cm) vivarium and when they are all coiled in the hide, their heads often pop out of the opening to survey the scene.

A pair of adults should be housed in an escape-proof vivarium measuring at least 36 x 18 x 15 in (90 x 45 x 38 cm). Make sure water is available at all times. Insert a humidity chamber. This is a box with a small opening that is filled with moistened moss or vermiculite—it has a high humidity in comparison to the rest of the environment. Alternatively, introduce a section of well-sprayed plastic plants to provide a suitably humid region. The temperature range should be maintained at 77–82°F (25–28°C).

HANDLING

One of the reasons I recommend purpose-built vivaria, instead of modified fish tanks, is that the best way to approach a snake is from the side

VIVARIUM SECURITY

A vivarium lock should be fitted to keep
your pet in and unwanted guests out.
A rubber wedge is also useful to stop the
doors sliding open if the unit is not locked.

Glass tanks and vivaria should be placed on
a sheet of polystyrene to insulate the glass
or wood, and prevent the base from
cracking or scratching furniture.

A circuit breaker should be fitted to any
electrical equipment—ask in-store personnel
or check with a qualified electrician.

▲ **In this artificial snake hide wait two young
House Snakes. Much of their time is spent
concealed in this way.**

rather than from above. Many predators attack
from above and the snake may not have time to
"smell" or "see" your hand before striking out at
this predatory movement. Front opening vivaria
will eliminate this worry and they are also likely to
be more escape-proof than converted aquaria.

Start to handle your snake as soon as you get it.
House Snakes are, in my opinion, well suited to
handling as a pet, although they will bite if your
fingers are wiggled about like a pinkie in front of
their noses.

FOODS AND FEEDING

Feeding is rarely a problem as these are greedy
snakes that always seem to be hungry or willing
to feed. House Snakes are capable of taking quite
large prey in relation to their head and neck size.
They tend to be good feeders and rarely refuse
food, or fast, which is not uncommon in other
species. In general, hatchlings should be offered
a couple of small pinkies every 3–4 days. Feed
juveniles 2–3 pinkies or furries every 6–8 days
and adults 1–3 adult mice every 10–14 days.

BREEDING

A female House Snake may lay between 8–15
eggs per clutch. Any discolored or wrinkled
eggs should be removed and the remaining
ones incubated at 80°F (26.5°C). Eggs should
hatch after approximately 60 days into babies
measuring on average 8 in (20.5 cm) in length.
Each hatchling can be fed a pinky after one week
of birth, but make sure all the snakes obtain
their fair share of food. Raise the young in small,
escape-proof containers. Baby snakes can
escape from the tiniest hole or curl up and hide
in the smallest piece of cork and will be hard to
spot by the untrained eye.

A juvenile House Snake should be purchased
when it is at least 8–12 in (20–30 cm) long. It
may initially be kept in a fairly small pet home,
heated using a heating pad. Once it starts to
grow, move it to a 24 x 15 x 15 in (60 x 38 x 38
cm) vivarium (this unit is suitable for up to 6–9
months) or straight into a 36 x 15 x 15 in
(90 x 38 x 38 cm) vivarium that will still be
large enough once your snake is fully grown.

BALL PYTHONS

Python regius

In the wild these snakes may be spotted at dawn or dusk, hunting or waiting to ambush their favorite food—the "jumping mouse" or gerbil. Once seized, their prey is suffocated and swallowed whole.

Occurring in west and central African grasslands and forest clearings, Ball Pythons are small and thick-set, measuring on average 39 in (100 cm) in length, although a mature female may exceed 78 in (200 cm). This species is familiar to hobbyists because its size and docility make it a perfect vivarium pet. In captivity they prefer a dimly lit setup and shy away from intense light.

▲ This Ball is now the right size to start handling. They are smaller, more manageable, and more suitable as pets than other pythons.

CREATING THE RIGHT ENVIRONMENT

For a single mature specimen a 48 x 18 x 18 in (120 x 45 x 45 cm) vivarium is a minimum requirement. It should be well-ventilated and have front-sliding doors for access. The temperature should be maintained at 75–85°F (24–29.5°C). Provide shelter in the form of logs, rocks, or natural cork to create resting areas for the snake. Wood chips, leaf litter, or plain paper can be used as substrate. Your snake will appreciate a good-sized water bowl.

Keep the vivarium relatively dry but mist spray periodically with warm water. This is especially helpful for the python when it is ready to shed its skin because the increased humidity helps to lubricate the old skin.

HANDLING

Ball Pythons are usually very easy to handle. Their initial eagerness to curl up into a ball disappears once they accept that you pose no threat or danger. They are nervous and tend to back away from any initial contact, but will very rarely bite. The name Ball Python was given because of its hedgehog-like habit of curling into a ball shape when threatened. As a stout snake, its body weight should be supported at all times.

Short stocky snakes rarely climb, and the Ball Python is almost exclusively terrestrial

Bold mottled patterns camouflage pythons in dappled sunlight of forest clearings

A row of special heat-sensitive pits help pythons to detect and capture prey effectively

▲ Passive and shy, Ball Pythons are a very inoffensive and popular species. They are solid looking, heavier, and more rotund than many other species of snake.

AMAZING FACT

Pythons are regarded by some African tribes as the Spirit of Rivers, God of War, and Goddess of Fertility, often being kept in shrines. At one time in the State of Dahomey sailors in the early days of th British Empire were put to death for harming them.

FOODS AND FEEDING

Ball Pythons have a well documented tendency to fast in captivity. There may be several reasons for this strange behavior. It is more than likely that a recently moved or imported specimen will not eat until it has settled and is comfortable in its new home, so allow a few weeks for this acclimatization to take place.

A lack of appetite may also be due to the wrong foodstuffs being offered at the wrong time of the day. From experience, I have found that the easiest way to start these pythons feeding is to allow them approximately two weeks to settle in to their new environment and then early one evening (reduce lighting, if necessary) offer a dead gerbil or a brown mouse. If this is refused, remove it after 30 minutes or so and try again a few days later. If your offering is not accepted, you may wish to offer another dead, but warm, specimen. In this way, an older snake can be weaned off live food. Of course, not all snakes will be so willing.

In captivity, the record held for a fasting Ball Python is probably 26 months, with only water being taken during this period. Should a well-fed Ball Python stop feeding for several weeks do not worry unduly—this seems to be perfectly normal behavior. In due course, the snake will feed again.

A baby farmed python will usually accept warmed prey readily but if it needs encouragement, try wiggling the food about on long tweezers. I have known many Ball Pythons who feed with astonishing appetites on dead mice, rats, sparrows, pinkies, and fuzzies, and on one occasion a piece of raw chicken started a stubborn individual feeding.

When ready to feed, your python may eat two or more mice per week. It is just as likely, however, to eat nothing for a couple of months. When cooling pythons for breeding, courtship and for gravid females, consumption of food can be virtually nil.

◄ **The coloration of a Ball Python is very appealing. Color morphs include xanthic, striped, albino, and a variable form called piebald. The popularity of the Ball Python has made these morphs very profitable.**

▼ The two claws visible on either side of the vent are, in effect, the remains of rear legs from distant ancestors.

DEFENSE MECHANISM

When threatened, the majority of snakes will either flee or fight back. Most unusually for a snake, however, the Ball Python simply coils itself into a tight ball and hopes that its compact shape will deter any would-be predators.

BREEDING

There are very few Ball Pythons that are bred in captivity. Most of the available specimens are either farmed or ranched in West African countries such as Nigeria or Ghana.

In the wild, pythons consume vast quantities of vermin and this helps to keep stored grain safe and dwellings rat-free. In return for this valuable assistance, the native peoples gather gravid females together and then harvest the young once they have hatched. If the females are released into the wild, this type of snake farming must be seen as a positive move. But usually both the females and their young are shipped overseas.

Males and females are distinguished by two claws visible on either side of the vent. These are, in effect, the remains of rear legs from distant ancestors—snakes are the last group of reptiles to have evolved. These claws are larger in males and are used to stimulate the female during courtship.

Mature, active Ball Pythons will mate and lay between 6–8 eggs above ground. These eggs are guarded and are partially incubated by one of the parent snakes. The parent remains coiled around the eggs until they hatch, usually about 100 days later if kept warm—about 86°F (30°C).

Newly hatched Balls will rarely accept a feed until after their first shed (approximately 8 days after hatching). They are normally quick and eager feeders and possess a beautiful golden hue that is present only for the first few months of life.

▼ Snakes have no eardrums. Instead, a vibration-transmitting bone is connected to the lower jaw. They are largely deaf to airborne sound but may "feel" vibrations from the ground.

COMMON GARTER SNAKE

Thamnophis sirtalis

This diurnal snake is native to North and Central America. Garters are often exported to Europe where they are considered exotic.

In the wild, Garter Snakes are generally found near water and feed mainly on amphibians, including tadpoles, frogs, fish, and earthworms. Many subspecies of this highly variable snake exist. Some of these inhabit drier regions and are more likely to take pinkies and mice than those from wetter habitats.

This is a slender and active species of snake that grows to 24–48 in (60–120 cm) in length. In captivity, they may live for 8–10 years— a natural life span in the wild would be considerably less.

CREATING THE RIGHT ENVIRONMENT

A 36 x 15 x 15 in (90 x 38 x 38 cm) vivarium will suit an adult pair of Garter Snakes. They generally require a dry vivarium furnished with a humidity box and a large water bowl. Reptile grass or even paper can be used as a substrate, but regularly changed wood chips or larger stones are more attractive options. Logs, branches, and other furnishings can provide an attractive home for a Garter Snake. The vivarium should offer plenty of hiding

places and a good range of temperatures to allow your snake to thermoregulate. Keep temperatures in the range of 68–79°F (20–26°C) during the summer months and lower to 50°F (10°C) in winter. Those from the extreme northern part of the range are active for only 3 months of the year. Follow a good hygiene regime. Keep substrates

A Garter Snake's scales are "keeled" with a central ridge

Tail length in snakes is measured from the vent to the tail tip— males have longer tails than females

These snakes are characterized by short snouts and eyes with round pupils

▲ Most Garter Snakes are excellent swimmers and hunt much of their prey in and around ponds, streams, and rivers.

dry and clean to reduce the chance of bacteria multiplying—undertank heaters are ideal for keeping substrates dry. Use a thermometer to check temperature and a thermostat is recommended to maintain an optimum temperature gradient.

HANDLING

Garter Snakes handle well after initial training. Younger ones, especially juveniles raised in captivity, are most likely to remain calm when handled and can be fed carefully from the fingers or with long tweezers.

Ribbon Snakes
Thamnophis sp

Ribbon and Garter Snakes look very similar and are members of the same genus. Ribbon Snakes have longer, more streamlined bodies and are able to cover open ground faster than Garters. Care conditions are virtually identical, but Ribbon Snakes will rarely eat earthworms, preferring tree frogs and other amphibians and fish for the bulk of their diet. Breeding is only likely if a group is kept together communally. Litters are small, with 4–5 young being born in early summer. They are rarely available from captive-bred stocks.

FOODS AND FEEDING

Garters require more regular feeds than many other species of snake and should be fed every other day. Fish, fish pieces, earthworms, pinkies, and small mice can be offered. Commercial snake foods in a can are also available.

It may be necessary to wiggle food around, especially to begin with, to stimulate a feeding response in your snake. It is well known that a diet of dead fish can cause a deficiency in thiamine (Vitamin B1), so fish pieces will need to be dusted with vitamin supplements. The processed "garter" foods are supplemented to overcome this potential problem. Supplying a varied diet is the key to maintaining optimum health in this particular species.

BREEDING

Garter snakes are live-bearers and the young grow rapidly if fed correctly, maturing at 8–10 months of age. The number of young can vary between subspecies and depends on the age, experience, and health of the female. Between 10–80 young per litter is typical. Sperm is retained by females and they may produce young up to two years after one successful mating.

AMAZING FACT

Garter Snakes rely greatly on their sight for hunting. As a diurnal predator they can track by sight and scent, seizing their prey firmly in the mouth. Prey is generally too small to need constriction and the majority of animals are swallowed head first.

Invertebrates

We share our world with millions of invertebrates. They are the basis of many food chains and are the most abundant creatures on the planet. Predatory mantids and leaf-crunching stick insects are examples of these fascinating creatures.

Ninety-seven percent of all living animals are invertebrates, that is, creatures that do not possess a backbone. These include lice, fleas, giant clams, and squid. Some invertebrates have a special body structure called an exoskeleton, which is a hard external structure as seen on a scorpion or millipede. Other species, such as worms, are composed of soft tissues.

All invertebrates are ectotherms, which means that they are reliant on external sources of temperature to maintain their bodily functions. Interestingly, newly discovered species have been found to thrive under extreme environmental conditions, both above and below what scientists have conventionally termed fatal temperatures—for example, under ice caps and at thermal vents.

Many invertebrates, especially those that attack crops or invade homes, are in conflict with humans. For example, millions of dollars are spent on researching new methods of control for malaria-carrying mosquitoes, *Anopheles sp* and the potato-attacking Colorado beetle, *Leptinotarsa decemlineata*. Other species, such as the honey bee, *Apis sp*, are beneficial since they produce tons of honey and wax, and pollinate fruit trees.

Invertebrates consume a variety of foodstuffs. Some species, such as spiders and scorpions, are carnivores, while others, such as stick and leaf insects, are herbivores. Cockroaches are

scavengers, willing to consume anything offered. Foodstuffs are obtained in a variety of ways and may be grazed, hunted, ambushed, trapped, snared, or lured, depending on the individual species of invertebrate.

Among the thousands of known species there is an enormous range of reproductive strategies to ensure the continued survival of this diverse group of animals. Many species produce eggs after completing a mating embrace, some are parthenogenic (unmated females producing fertile eggs), and most mollusks, including snails, are hermaphrodites.

In general, invertebrates are the least handleable of all the exotic creatures in this book. If you are in any doubt, do not handle them. They should not be moved or handled during a molt, since they are extremely vulnerable to damage at this particular stage. Soon after a molt an invertebrate's body hardens and it can then be handled if necessary. Adult supervision is essential when young hobbyists wish to move or handle these creatures.

▶ **Praying mantids are short-lived predatory invertebrates found in Europe, the Americas, and most tropical regions of the world.**

Only a few invertebrate species are suitable to keep as household pets. Some are familiar to us all—insects, for example, which have six legs, a body split into three sections, and an exoskeleton. These are the most numerous of all creatures on the planet—a large swarm of a single insect species, such as locusts, may contain more individual insects than the entire human population.

Some invertebrates are very attractive and, although somewhat unusual, are fast becoming desirable pets. Insects generally require little space (stick and leaf insects, for example) and are easy to maintain. They have fascinating life cycles and behavior patterns that make them educational pets.

▲ The spider's internal structure is visible in this recently shed tarantula skin. Adults molt once or twice a year to enable them to grow and renew lost or damaged limbs. Spiders are frequently very hungry and thirsty after a molt.

INVERTEBRATE CLASSIFICATION (EXTRACT)

Class	Description	No. of Species
INSECTA	Invertebrates in this class typically have three pairs of legs and are the only invertebrates to have wings as adults. Praying mantids belong to the order DICTYOPTERA and over 6000 species are known to man. Stick and leaf insects belong to the order PHASMIDA and there are approximately 2000 known species.	approximately 800,000
ARACHNID	These creatures have four pairs of legs and the body is normally made up of two parts, with a thin "waist" separating the cephalothorax (head) and the abdomen (body). Tarantulas belong to the sub-order ORTHOGNATHA and scorpions belong to the order SCORPIONIDAE.	approximately 70,000
MYRIAPODA	Millipedes and centipedes belong to this group of animals. Millipedes are inoffensive scavengers. Their legs are contained under the body, which is often black, brown, or delicately striped.	approximately 11,000

INDIAN STICK INSECT

Carausius morosus

Although still considered exotic, this species has been kept in England for over 100 years, but special permits may be required in some states.

Indian Stick Insects are one of the easiest species of invertebrates to manage. Their bodies range from green to brown in color and they possess bright red spots on the inside of their forelegs that are flashed as a warning when they are disturbed. If threatened, they will often drop to the ground and remain motionless like a twig. When the danger has passed, they will open their legs and start to move again. Once adult, female stick insects measure up to 4½ in (11 cm). Males are rarely encountered. Life expectancy is approximately one year.

CREATING THE RIGHT ENVIRONMENT

Requiring a tall vivarium, measuring at least 12 x 18 x 12 in (30 x 45 x 30 cm), these insects will live mostly on their food plant. These should be potted up and changed regularly to ensure an abundant food supply. Fresh cut sprigs of privet or leafy lengths of bramble can be used, but unpotted plants will dry quickly and be of little benefit to your pets unless replaced often.

Keeping your insects at a temperature of 75°F (24°C) is ideal, but they are very tolerant and will be happy in a warm room. A reasonable level of humidity is required—regularly mist sprayed but ensure good ventilation to prevent molds from growing. Thirsty stick insects exercise their mouth parts continuously and a quick spray of droplets onto a leaf soon quenches their thirst. Cover the floor of the unit in paper so that any eggs that have been laid are readily visible. Cleaning is minimal— just change the paper weekly.

Giant Spiny Stick Insect

Eurycantha calcarata

A large chocolate brown species, with females growing to 6 in (15 cm) and males to 4 in (10 cm), they are well armored, especially the males who are equipped with two large, sharp spurs on the legs to fight off rivals. Only females have an ovipositor. The nymphs vary from orange to green in color. This species spends most of its time resting, often in large numbers, in logs, or behind tree bark. More ground space is therefore required and a well-ventilated 24 in (60 cm) cubed vivarium is ideal. This species loves water and will drink quite often. A shallow saucer of water should be offered on a regular basis. Handle your pet with great care—lift from underneath using the palm of your hand.

HANDLING

These little creatures tame easily but need to be handled with great care. Gently pick up your insect between finger and thumb, or offer a flat palm, and tap it so that it walks onto your hand. Legs that are stuck or hooked onto an object or piece of clothing need a gentle nudge to loosen their grip.

A classic insect, with six legs and a body divided into three parts: the head, thorax, and abdomen

Antennae are covered in tiny sensory hairs to help the insect understand its environment

Privet is an easy plant to grow and can be propagated into small pots suitable for the vivarium

FOODS AND FEEDING

They are herbivorous by nature, eating only plant material throughout their lives. Privet and bramble are their favorite foods. You can plant these in your garden at little or no cost and provide your pet with a lifetime's supply of food. However, make sure you do not release the insects into your garden.

BREEDING

Stick insects are parthenogenetic, capable of reproducing without mating. Adult female Indian Stick Insects lay fertilized eggs measuring about .08 in (2 mm). Hundreds of these tiny eggs will be laid during her lifetime, several a day during peak output. These smooth round "pods" are easily separated from droppings if further young are required. Place them on sand or vermiculite in a clear tub and leave in a warm place. Remember to check them periodically.

The young can take up to a year to hatch and require identical vivarium conditions to adults, but they must not be overcrowded because they will eat each other's legs. As babies appear, place them in a rearing container supplied with plenty of new leaves for them to feast on.

A baby stick insect, or nymph, will grow to adulthood within a few months by molting six times. While molting they will suspend themselves from vegetation or the container lid. During this stage they are extremely vulnerable and should be left alone to drop out of their old skin and harden their new one before handling. The old skin will usually be eaten.

◄ **Many species of stick insect can be kept under similar conditions. Simple to keep, they are a good introduction to keeping invertebrates.**

LEAF INSECTS

Phyllium sp

Their bodies are generally flat and green. Brown "tatty" edges and the odd hole complete the camouflage. Some states require special permits to keep these insects.

The Leaf Insect is native to the warm and humid Malaysian jungles and, depending on the species, will measure 3–6 in (8–15 cm) once adult. It is shorter lived (6–8 months) and more difficult to maintain and breed than stick insects, but it is undoubtedly worth the extra effort.

CREATING THE RIGHT ENVIRONMENT

A 24 x 18 x 12 in (60 x 45 x 30 cm) vivarium will house up to 6 individuals. While preferring temperatures in the region of 70–80°F (21–27°C), they do not like stagnant air, so good ventilation is essential for optimum growth and development, especially during a molt. Maintain the temperature within the vivarium using undertank heaters or keep it in the warmest part of the home.

Since leaf insects are arboreal creatures the choice of substrate is largely decorative. However, plain paper should be placed on the base of the vivarium when they are breeding so that eggs may easily be located. Wood chips, or even moss, kept moist would help to keep humidity at around 70%. Regular mist spraying with tepid water and use of a hygrometer is recommended. In captivity, Leaf Insects both live and feed on bramble leaves. Replace sprigs daily or place potted plants in the vivarium. These insects need to climb.

The thorax contains muscles that operate the three pairs of legs

Antennae are covered in tiny sensory hairs

Compound eyes are made up of many lenses—most insects have good eyesight and perceive color

▲ Leaf Insects are worth the effort that is required to keep and breed a colony in captivity. This sub-adult is almost ready for breeding.

HANDLING

Adults may be encouraged to walk onto your hand. They wobble about in a highly comical fashion trying to convince you that they are a leaf blowing in the breeze. Handle them with care because it is so easy to damage these very delicate creatures.

FEEDING

Leaf Insects are herbivorous. They eat Guava and other tropical leaves in the jungle but, in captivity, they will accept bramble leaves as a substitute. Fresh sprigs should be inserted into the vivarium every other day or so; alternatively, pot up a few small plants.

BREEDING

These small invertebrates have a life expectancy measured in months, not years, and at about 4–5 months of age they are ready to mate. Males are easily identified by their slimmer bodies and longer wings.

About 100 eggs are produced singly. These drop to the ground and are camouflaged to look like the droppings of a silk moth caterpillar living in the same region in the wild. A few weeks after the eggs are laid the parents die. Incubate the eggs in the same way as Stick Insect eggs.The babies are bright red and will immediately climb up into bushes and start feeding on leaves.

Leaf Insects rely totally on camouflage— they cannot bite or fight an attacker

Insects have no lungs and breathe through tiny holes in the body called spiracles

▲ Insects excel at camouflage and the detailed design and color of the Leaf Insect would make spotting one in the wild a remarkable achievement.

GIANT MILLIPEDES

Epibolus sp

There are about 8,000 recorded species of millipede. Commonly called "jungle trains" or "chongaloloo" in Africa, several different varieties are now available to the hobbyist.

These are essentially animals of soil and leaf litter. They are easy to establish and it is quite possible to breed them providing several are kept together as a colony. They may be reddish-brown or black, and some species are even striped. Growing to 10 in (25 cm) in length, they can live for several years if they are kept in the right conditions. Millipedes are slow, harmless scavengers and should not be confused with centipedes.

CREATING THE RIGHT ENVIRONMENT

A large container is necessary. One measuring either 36 x 18 x 12 in (90 x 45 x 30 cm) or 24 x 12 x 12 in (60 x 30 x 30 cm) will make a suitable home. Add chemical-free compost, or peat moss, to a depth of 2^1/$_2$–3 in (6–8 cm) and cover with a quantity of leaf litter—oak, sycamore, and moss are ideal. It is advisable to pre-freeze leaf litter to kill unwanted mini-beasts that may colonize your millipede's home. Logs and small pieces of cork chip are used to cover the soil and provide grazing. Maintain a temperature of 75–80°F (24–27°C) using an undertank heater. Mist occasionally to keep humid, but make sure it is not too damp or wet.

You only need to clean out your vivarium 1–2 times a year. If you keep a large number of millipedes together, you will need to do this more often. All compost should be disposed of and replaced.

HANDLING

Millipedes are active at night or under crepuscular conditions. Many species can secrete unpleasant fluids from glands along the sides of the body when disturbed or offended. These may smell, sting, or stain clothing. When disturbed they will coil up tightly for protection. They will also curl up when at rest or sleeping.

Millipedes have a delicate central nervous system and a small fall can kill them

When alarmed, they curl up tightly to protect their vulnerable legs from attack

Tiny hooks on every leg enable the millipede to grasp and move across many surfaces

Frequently handled specimens stop secreting these fluids because they know you will not harm them. Some people do wear gloves, but the main thing is to treat these invertebrates with respect and learn to enjoy their company.

▼ The name millipede, meaning "thousand feet," is an exaggeration. No species has many more than 300 legs.

Florida Millipede
Chicobolus spinigerus

This 3–5 in (8–13 cm) species is attractively marked and found in the Southeast, namely from Florida and northwards into South Carolina. They should be kept at temperatures of 70–80°F (21–27°C) in the same conditions as Giant Millipedes. Numerous native American species of millipede exist, but few are as large as those imported from the tropics. Temperate countries like Great Britain have tiny millipedes rarely exceeding a few centimeters in length.

FOODS AND FEEDING

Besides eating leaf litter, small cubed pieces of vegetable and fruit may be offered to your pet on upturned jelly jar lids or small saucers. These should be removed every few days, and you will soon get an idea of what your particular millipede likes. Millipede waste appears in the form of small fecal pellets and it can be removed occasionally from the vivarium; it makes excellent compost for plants. As the leaf litter in their home disappears it will need to be replenished.

BREEDING

Males are easily sexed when viewed from underneath—gonopods are visible on the seventh or eighth segment. These are modified legs used to transfer sperm to the females. In a male millipede these modified legs are frequently hidden from view.

Millipedes wrap around each other to mate. Some then build a nest in which to lay eggs. Should yours breed, you will soon notice numerous babies crawling about the leaf litter. Under a magnifying glass these can be seen to have much fewer segments and legs. There is no need to move them to a separate rearing container since they will be quite safe with Mom and Dad, soon developing more legs.

▲ Each measuring only 2½ in (6 cm) in length, this trio of young captive-bred millipedes is ready to start a new colony.

PRAYING MANTIS

Sphodromantis sp

The first part of its name describes well the mantis' famous pose, with forelimbs raised up to its head as if in prayer. It is also one of the few insects that can turn its head and "look over its shoulder."

There are about 2,000 species of Praying Mantis worldwide; several are native to the U.S. Most of them are found in the tropics but some are native to Europe. At least one European species, *Mantis religiosa*, was introduced into the United States early in the twentieth century by accident, and is now widespread and considered a naturalized species. Several are available from pet stores but many more through membership of relevant specialist societies.

Generally green or brown in color, one particularly attractive species, the Orchid Praying Mantis, *Hymenopus coronatus*, is a shade of pink closely resembling the flower blooms it rests upon while awaiting insect visitors.

The Praying Mantis is a voracious predator. It will actively stalk its prey or else wait patiently, camouflaged against foliage, for an insect to venture within striking range. Upon close examination we can see that mantids are well designed for killing. The long front legs are lined with numerous spines and a curved hook which, in a fraction of a second, snatches and impales the unsuspecting insect. Once held, the prey's fate is sealed and the mantis starts to consume it alive.

Your pet mantis will usually grow to 3 in (7.5 cm) in length and will live for approximately one year.

CREATING THE RIGHT ENVIRONMENT

Praying Mantids are generally purchased as nymphs, individually packed in small plastic containers covered with netting or punctured with tiny breathing holes. Measuring only about 3/4 in (2 cm) in length, your mantis will reside on a twig or other object upon which it can climb. As long as it is fed on fruit flies or other tiny prey and is kept warm at 75°F (24°C), this small space will be sufficient for a while. As the mantis feeds and

▲ **Young mantids are reared separately in small containers. Simple to keep and with a life span of one year, they are a short-term commitment.**

needs to grow it will molt, reaching its next development stage (known as an instar). Having molted several times, larger accommodation should be offered.

After 5–6 molts, your Praying Mantis will reach adulthood. Probably measuring no more than 3 in (7.5 cm), a 24 x 18 x 12 in (60 x 45 x 30 cm) vivarium or a tall unit measuring 12 x 18 x 12 in (30 x 45 x 30 cm) will be ideal. Anything larger than this and you might not be able to see and enjoy your pet, so effective is its camouflage. A daytime temperature of 75°F (24°C) is best— an undertank heater will do this for you. This can drop by a few degrees at night with no ill effects. Housing should be well ventilated. Mantids should be kept individually because they are just as happy to eat one another as to eat their normal prey.

As arboreal invertebrates, mantids need to be provided with something to climb upon.Branches, twigs, foliage, and other decoration will provide this and make an attractive home for you and your mantis to enjoy. A living plant really helps to enhance a display, but do ensure that the light bulb is not positioned too close to it. Perhaps consider using a full spectrum fluorescent light instead to maintain plant health.

▼ **A voracious predator, the Praying Mantis is a glutton, forever on the lookout for unwary prey.**

The forelegs are specially formed for impaling and holding live prey

The eyes are large, vision is good, and the head turns to follow movement

Six visible segments on the abdomen indicate that this is a female

▲ **Praying Mantids are usually green like this attractive specimen, but some varieties mimic colorful flowers or even dead leaves found on the forest floor.**

HANDLING

For close examination you can encourage a mantis onto the palm of your hand, where it will move around from hand to hand quite happily. Don't attempt to pick one up using your finger and thumb because the mantis will jab you with its forearms. Mantids can fly, so ensure windows and doors are closed before allowing a mantis to climb on your hand.

AMAZING FACT

Many Kung Fu moves are derived from the movements of the Praying Mantis. 400 years ago Wang Lang, already a martial arts expert, was inspired while watching a mantis kill a cicada. He developed his style using a refined series of moves mimicking the mantis' ability to strike and grab.

INSTARS & MOLTING

An instar is a development stage, and the number it takes to reach adulthood depends on the species. Molting is the process between instars enabling growth and development to take place.

FOODS AND FEEDING

A mantis will eat almost any live foods that it can catch and hold in its powerful forelegs. The youngest will eat fruit flies, but once they begin to grow they will quickly graduate to katydids, crickets, butterflies, grasshoppers, and flies. In the wild, even bees and wasps will be eaten. Feed your pet as much as it will eat. Leave a few suitably sized prey insects in the vivarium so that your mantis can feed whenever it is hungry.

They are messy feeders, leaving discarded legs, wings, and other body parts lying around the vivarium floor. These should be removed on a regular basis and, apart from removing fecal pellets, this is the only cleaning required.

Your mantis may drink the odd drop of water direct from leaves and should be sprayed with water every day or so. Make sure that your vivarium is airy and well ventilated.

BREEDING

Mantids are essentially an annual species, with offspring emerging each spring. If lucky, they survive to mature, mate and, if female, lay eggs before dying within the same year. Your pet mantis is therefore relatively short lived, taking six months to mature and then living for approximately six months as an adult. By growing on several nymphs to maturity, you have a good chance of breeding them.

▲ Baby mantids are protected before hatching by the hardened foam exterior of their egg case.

Females are easily distinguished from males. They have six visible segments on the underside of their abdomen, while males have eight. Mating is a dangerous time for males—they may be eaten attempting to mate, during mating, or immediately afterwards. One female may produce several egg cases, or oothecae, from a successful mating. Even unmated females will lay eggs, but these will not hatch.

The new generation emerges in great numbers from each egg case, which may contain 20–200 eggs. Newly emerged mantids are the size of a mosquito and are miniature versions of the adults. Like all insects, by the time they have reached adulthood they have wings and can fly. The appearance of wings establishes that maturity has been reached and that the mantids are ready to breed.

TARANTULAS

Family: Theraphosidae

There are approximately 800 species of tarantula. They are large and hairy, often possessing interesting colors and markings. Tarantulas are predators and have large fangs.

No record can be found of human deaths caused by a tarantula bite—they are not considered a species dangerous to man. Tarantulas are popular and can be very low cost pets, requiring only the minimum of time and space to maintain in excellent condition. Bred in large quantities, it is recommended that you purchase one of the test-tube reared spiderlings measuring between 1/2–3/4 in (1–2 cm). The most popular species bred and kept in captivity come from North, Central, and South America. One of these is the Curly-haired Tarantula, *Brachypelma albopilosa*, my personal favorite ("Erica" is shown below).

A cluster of eight eyes on the cephalothorax (or head)

Spinnerets produce silk

Pedipalps help the spider smell, taste, and feel

Two hollow fangs inject venom—these are hidden from view by the chelicerae, or mouth parts

▲ Tarantulas can be handled on a daily basis without any incidents occuring. Their dangerous image belies their gentle nature.

Hooks enable tarantulas to get a good grip on slippery surfaces

110

▲ **This double spider unit safely separates two adult tarantulas.**

CREATING THE RIGHT ENVIRONMENT

Most species of tarantula should be kept singly in glass containers. House spiderlings in small jars or plastic containers and increase the container size as the spider grows. A 12 x 12 x 8 in (30 x 30 x 20 cm) unit is sufficient to house a single adult for its entire life, although a large vivarium measuring 24 x 12 x 12 in (60 x 30 x 30 cm) or 36 x 12 x 12 in (90 x 30 x 30 cm) may be used to create a more natural-looking landscape.

Care must be taken with larger units, however, to ensure that a high enough humidity level is

Chilean Rose Tarantula
Grammostola cala

This popular species has a salmon-pink hue and is one of the best spiders to keep with a view to occasional handling—experienced adult supervision is required. Like most species of tarantula, it should be kept singly, except for breeding purposes.

maintained. The experience of numerous tarantula breeders and keepers shows us that smaller units appear to be more beneficial to most species—they often spend days, or even weeks, squeezed into "burrows" the size of empty toilet rolls within the vivarium. A hygrometer will help you to measure humidity levels accurately. Desert species require 50%–70% relative humidity and tropical species need 70%–90% relative humidity in order to breathe.

Glass spider tanks are available and these help to keep the humidity levels high. Fine ventilation mesh ensures that the air does not stagnate. These glass units are preferable to over-ventilated plastic aquariums. The majority of species are ground dwelling and they require a good quality substrate and a cork "cave," burrow, or similar shelter. The base should be covered with substrate to a depth of 3–4 in (8–10 cm); peat moss, vermiculite, or a mixture of both should be thoroughly dampened to provide ideal conditions. A cork log or similar shelter should be leaned in one corner for aboreal species. Maintain the temperature at 75°F–84°F (24–29°C).

A unit containing a solitary tarantula requires virtually no cleaning—maybe only once a year. When cleaning out the vivarium, it is best to "usher" your spider into an escape-proof pot or tub for easy and safe removal. The vermiculite or other substrate should be disposed of and cork or other loose objects cleaned thoroughly. Never use disinfectants, insecticides, or bleach; boiling water will be sufficient. Freezing cork or logs is another way to minimize the risk of introducing unwanted pests into your vivarium.

HANDLING

The best advice I can give is never to handle your pet spider. Many people, however, wish to experience the thrill of such intimacy. If you are intent on trying to hold one, the following information should be taken into account. Handling a tarantula should only be attempted when an experienced adult is on hand to assist. These spiders have large fangs that will definitely hurt if you are bitten, and their venom is similar in strength to that of a bee sting. Many people are allergic to venoms, and bee venom kills more people annually than any other venomous creature. Some species of tarantula, such as the Curly-haired or Chilean Rose, seem to be the most passive and friendly in my experience. Handling any spider is not recommended for people of a nervous disposition.

Never handle your pet during, just before or after a molt, or just after feeding. Start handling your spider when it is still young by gently encouraging it to walk onto your hand from its vivarium, or from a flat surface such as a low table. You should be sitting down on the floor, so that if you get scared and drop the spider, or the spider gets scared and jumps off you, serious injury from a fall onto a hard surface can be avoided. Do not put your tarantula close to your face or eyes just in case it rubs off some hairs, which can cause irritation.

As soon as a tarantula appears agitated or "rubs hairs," stop handling it. A tarantula may defecate on you; it does not hurt, but can give some people a shock. Don't let your tarantula crawl onto clothing because the tiny claws on each leg may get caught and stuck in the fibers. Never handle Asian Bird-eating Tarantulas or specimens of the *Poecilotheria* sp. A person was once hospitalized after a bite from an unidentified *Poecilotheria* species in Sri Lanka.

▲ **People get a thrill from handling tarantulas. However, such close contact is best left for experienced individuals to teach the uninitiated.**

FOODS AND FEEDING

All species of tarantula, ranging from juveniles to adults, can be reared on insects but the size of prey should reflect the capacity of the spider. Make sure you offer a variety of food types.

Young tarantulas (spiderlings) will feed on hatchling crickets or fruit flies (especially flightless ones), and as the spiderling grows and molts, larger prey should be offered. On average, foods should be approximately a quarter to one-third the length of the spider. You will soon see, if observant, what size or type of prey is attractive to your pet.

Pink-toed Tarantula
Avicularia avicularia

This non-aggressive arboreal species is a fast moving and very attractive fuzzy black spider with pink "toes." A 24-in (60-cm) cubed vivarium would make a lovely display unit for 4–5 of these "social" tarantulas. Spiders of similar size may be kept together and cork logs, branches, or other climbable structures should be included in the setup. These spiders require 70%–80% humidity and a temperature range of 75–82°F (24–28°C). They build hammock-like webs, creating an interesting visual display. When several inhabitants are living together, lots of interaction is likely to be observed. A single specimen will be less active and may remain in seclusion for most of the day.

Crickets, mealworms, maggots, moths, and house flies are all potential food sources. Arboreal species of spider will prefer flying or climbing foods, whereas ground dwellers will prefer crickets, terrestrial bugs, and caterpillars. Offer your pet foods on a regular basis, at least twice a week to juveniles and every 9–11 days to more mature animals.

MOLTING

When your tarantula is found upside down or on its side in the vivarium, it is probably molting. Do not disturb it and carefully remove any live food still present. It can take between 1–2 days for an adult to complete the process. Spiderlings molt very regularly because they grow quickly. Adults do so less frequently and molt on average once a year.

Care must be taken to prevent the spider's unit from being overrun with uneaten live foods. These may annoy your tarantula or cause it terrible damage and stress if it begins to molt. Tarantulas refuse food prior to a molt, but are generally ravenous soon after. Long tweezers will help to remove any carcasses or uneaten prey without risking damage to your fingers. A well-fed tarantula, with a rounded abdomen, may only require infrequent feedings and will often eat nothing for weeks, or even months, at a time.

Spider venom is a specially modified digestive enzyme similar to, but more potent than, our own saliva. Its main use is to capture, kill, and pre-digest food; its defensive role is secondary.

In the wild most spiders obtain all the water they need from their humid environment and from food. In captivity it is a good idea, however, to have water available at all times.

BREEDING

Breeding tarantulas provides a fascinating insight into the precarious mating habits of spiders. You are, if successful, likely to feel euphoric at your achievement in helping to bring new lives into the world. However, before embarking upon this large venture, you might wish to consider whether you have a ready outlet for approximately 400–600 spiderlings and adequate time and energy to ensure their survival and development.

Initially, you will need to sex your spiders and to ensure that they are well fed, in particular the females. Male tarantulas mature after a particular molt; mating hooks will be visible near the joints on the underside of his front pair of legs. Once a male spider has matured, its life span can be measured in months. The odd individual may survive for a year. Female tarantulas tend to appear to be heavier and more rounded and have a larger abdomen. They may live 20 years.

An unhappy or threatened tarantula will release irritating hairs by rubbing its back legs against its abdomen (only New World species). This cloud of hairs floats into the air and onto the skin or face of their aggressor, causing a painful rash or temporary blindness.

▲ **This Asian Bird-eating Tarantula is very aggressive and has reared up into a threat posture. Any attempt to touch it would result in a bite. Spiders of the family Theraphosidae are usually more friendly.**

Mating carries considerable risks to male tarantulas—many are killed or badly injured in their attempt to mate with the longer-lived females. A male that is ready to mate will have deposited some sperm onto a small sheet of web. He will then dip his pedipalps into the sperm and proceed to visit a potential mate; a female releases an attractant scent that causes a male to seek her out.

If the male finds a willing partner, he will hold her fangs with his mating hooks and insert, and empty, his palps into her genital opening. You may, if things don't go according to plan, need to break in and separate them if fighting occurs. A plastic pet home is ideal to drop over each specimen without putting your fingers at risk. Once mating has taken place the male will retreat hastily to avoid becoming a post-nuptial meal.

Several days later the female will lay her eggs. Numbering into the hundreds, these are contained within a silk bag and protected by the mother until they hatch 8–10 weeks later into tiny colorless replicas of their parents. At this time, separate each spiderling into a tiny rearing container and feed it small live prey such as fruit flies. As they grow, they gradually acquire the markings of their parents. The parents, if both have survived, ought to be fed well to rebuild their strength if another mating attempt is to be made.

ASIAN BIRD EATERS

Native to Thailand and Southeast Asia, Asian Bird Eaters (a specimen is shown opposite) have attractive velvet markings on their bodies and lack the irritating hairs possessed by New World species of tarantula. Despite their name, these spiders mainly eat insects, such as crickets. They are rarely captive bred and are fast moving, very aggressive, and eager to bite—do not attempt to handle. This species is only suitable for the experienced tarantula keeper.

Mexican Red-kneed Tarantula
Brachypelma smithi

These are one of the most striking of all tarantulas—large in size and, as their name suggests, with bright red knees. This spider is a protected and threatened species. It is more expensive than other spiders and is available only from captive-bred stock. The females can be long lived—one has been recorded alive at 30 years of age.

I have in my collection four adult specimens. They were part of a seized shipment from Mexico, imported without the correct paperwork. Each spider lives in a unit measuring 8 x 8 x 8 in (20 x 20 x 20 cm) and I have had them for seven years. Ideal living conditions would consist of a 12 x 12 x 12 in (30 x 30 x 30 cm) vivarium, maintained at temperatures of 75–82°F (24–28°C) and 70% relative humidity.

This species is traditionally used for human contact at many zoos. However, I have found some individuals are easily annoyed and they will rub off their abdominal hairs at the slightest provocation.

IMPERIAL SCORPION

Pandinus imperator

**These creatures are native to the humid, tropical forests of
central Africa and spend much of their time under leaf litter
and in the cracks found in tree bark and fallen logs.**

The largest scorpion in the world, measuring
6 in (15 cm), may seem an unsuitable pet.
However, it is quite easy to care for and it is
not considered dangerous to humans. Living up
to 8 years, the Imperial Scorpion is occasionally
bred in captivity but is mainly imported from Africa.
This species is covered under CITES.

CREATING THE RIGHT ENVIRONMENT

This forest scorpion lives in burrows dug out
under rocks, logs, or other sturdy objects. Much
of its time will be spent beneath ground, only
venturing out after dark to hunt for food. Peat moss
or soil, 5–6 in (13–15 cm) deep, are ideal substrates
to place in the vivarium. Some parts should be

▲ Beauty or beast—scorpions are unusual pets that are easy to maintain in captivity.

◀ Compost, leaf litter, and cork bark, added to a depth of 5–6 in (13–15 cm), provide the correct environment for this scorpion. The acrylic vivarium is ideal—the lid fits securely and prevents your pet from escaping.

covered with wood, logs, and rocks but keep at least part of the ground clear so that the scorpion can move about freely.

Maintain the temperature at 77–86°F (25–30°C). Spray daily to maintain humidity and to provide an additional water source for these creatures, since they will also drink from drops on plastic plants or wood. Ground warmth is important for scorpions and an undertank heater should be placed under one third of the vivarium. A 24 x 12 x 12 in (60 x 30 x 30 cm) vivarium is fine for a single specimen.

A small colony of 4–10 individuals may be housed together for breeding purposes, as long as ample retreats and food are available. A vivarium measuring 48 x 12 x 12 in (120 x 30 x 30 cm) is adequate. Some fighting is inevitable within a small colony, and occasionally a specimen may be devoured by its "friends." For this reason many hobbyists prefer to keep specimens separately.

HANDLING

I do not recommend that novices or young people handle Scorpions. If you want to try, hold your pet firmly by its stinger and lift quickly onto your palm. This should only be done under experienced adult supervision. I hold my black scorpion regularly and have had no stings. However, the occasional pinch is to be expected. Beware though, some people are highly sensitive to insect venoms.

FOODS AND FEEDING

As predatory arachnids, these creatures prefer slow-moving prey such as large grubs and caterpillars. Dead mice, pinkies, and grasshoppers will also be accepted. Crickets, however, are generally too fast for the Imperial Scorpion to catch and may eventually establish themselves in the vivarium. Offer food twice weekly by releasing insects into the vivarium or by offering food, using long tweezers, directly to the scorpion.

BREEDING

Equipped with a pair of strong pincers and a poison gland in her tail, a potential female mate is approached by an amorous male with great caution. He swiftly grabs her pincers with his and, with her weapons safely checked, they start to dance, shuffling forwards and backwards. The male deposits a pack of sperm on the ground and as he pulls the female over it she takes up the pack into her body. To avoid becoming her supper, the male quickly relaxes his hold and they separate.

Eventually, some 20–50 live young appear as small white spots crawling on the mother's back. Within two weeks, once they have had their first molt and their exoskeletons have hardened, the babies leave the mother's back to fend for themselves. Maturing Imperial Scorpions shed their exoskeleton about once a year.

Preventing and Recognizing Exotic Pet Ailments

Prevention is the key. Most health problems can be prevented, since the major cause of herptile ill health is poor husbandry. A lack of proper hygiene and/or a bad feeding regime are largely responsible. By providing the correct environment with the right quantity and quality of foods most problems can be easily prevented.

I recommend that the novice purchases captive-bred specimens wherever possible. Imported, wild-caught species are more likely to suffer from internal and external parasites and bacterial infections. Many of these problems can be overcome with correct medication and laboratory style/quarantine housing. If you think you have problems of this nature, contact your reptile society or dealer for advice. Also, if you think your pet is sick or suffering, contact your veterinarian

or herptile veterinary specialist immediately. Most ailments that occur can be attributed to the environment, diet or injury caused by you or another animal, and are treatable.

OBESITY

One of the major general health problems of all pets is obesity. Too much food or a diet too high in preferred or fatty foods can cause serious problems. It is impossible to state exactly what quantity of each foodstuff should be given to any species, but try to imagine life in the wild where most species would not eat every day or all year round. Encourage activity in predatory herptiles by scattering food – this makes your animal "work" for its meal. This type of environmental enrichment is popular now in zoos. Dragging a defrosted mouse around the vivarium using long tweezers for a snake or releasing some bugs into the unit for a Leopard Gecko to physically stalk will aid this type of positive activity. Such "exercise" will help prevent your pet from becoming a "couch potato."

▲ **Obesity is one of the largest causes of ill health in pet animals – always feed in moderation.**

VITAMIN AND MINERAL SUPPLEMENTS

These are essential for many species but correct dosage is necessary since a lack, or excess, of vitamins and minerals can lead to problems. They are of particular importance for juveniles which are developing quickly. Follow manufacturers' guidelines for the duration of your pet's life.

METABOLIC BONE DISEASE

This disease is very common in herptiles whose diets have not been supplemented with vitamins and minerals. Reptiles need Vitamin D3 to absorb calcium to form healthy bones. There are a variety of products available and I would advise a fluorescent full-spectrum tube, with both UVA and UVB, or giving a powdered Vitamin D3 supplement.

ABSCESSES

Common in both snakes and lizards, an abscess may appear as a raised bump underneath the scales. Veterinarian treatment is required to surgically remove the infected swelling and to cleanse and suture the wound afterwards.

DEHYDRATION

The symptoms of dehydration are sunken eyes and remnants of unsuccessfully shed skin still attached to the body. In mild cases improve your pet's vivarium conditions. Mist spray and ensure that the animal drinks. Drying out (desiccation) can be avoided by offering a humidity chamber or raising the general humidity in the vivarium. Ensure that water bowls are sunk into the substrate to ground level to allow ease of access. Bad cases need veterinarian treatment quickly.

▲ **A simple humidity chamber can be made from a plastic dish filled with moistened moss or vermiculite to create a humid micro-climate.**

SHEDDING

Maintaining the right levels of humidity is one of the key factors in preventing problems when shedding (ecdysis). The inability to remove old skin properly is known as dysedysis and this can result in a restricted blood supply, especially to blood vessels around toes and fingers. A humidity chamber – a box containing plastic plants that are well sprayed – will help to reduce this problem in many species and will provide objects for your pet to rub against to aid shedding. Snakes do not eat their shed skin, but many lizards and amphibians will consume this nutritious material.

Common problems include: a spectacle (the clear scale over the eye) remaining on a snake – this can be removed carefully with a pair of tweezers; a tattered shed on a snake or lizard due to inadequate humidity – to remedy this, place your pet into a humidity chamber and/or remove the remains of the skin carefully by hand.

119

EXTERNAL PARASITES

Mites and ticks are common problems for reptiles. Mites are little pinhead-like objects that run about a reptile's scales while ticks burrow themselves underneath the scales, especially near the eyes, nostrils or vent. If you maintain good hygiene practices, you are unlikely to have a problem. Mites and ticks are controlled by using no-pest strips. Disinfect furnishings, wash the reptile and place a one-inch square in the vivarium for 24 hours, once a week, for three weeks. This should restrict if not eliminate the problem entirely. However, do not use near food insects or other pet insects!

BLISTERS

Especially common on Garter Snakes and other species inhabiting moist habitats. Blisters are caused by too humid of quarters. Clean the cage and replace with dry substrate. If the blisters persist, take your pet to a veterinarian.

INGESTED SUBSTRATE

This can cause major problems for herptiles. Provide food in dishes or bowls and try to ensure feeding animals do not take in this type of material when eating. Keeping an eye on your pet at meal times should prevent this type of problem.

EUTHANASIA

A terminally sick or aged specimen may need euthanasia. An overdose of barbituates is the most humane method and this should only be administered by a vet.

AMPHIBIANS AND BACTERIAL INFECTION

Bacterial infections are most common in amphibians because of their delicate skin and aquatic lifestyles. Dead foodstuffs and fecal matter should be removed regularly. Water quality is essential to maintain long-term health in captivity – water should be partly changed regularly. External filtration is always recommended and is probably the single most effective tool in preventing infections in aquatic and semi-aquatic animals. Numerous products are available in the pet trade to filter or condition water for aquatic species. Ensure that any product you purchase is suitable for the species you intend to use it on. All equipment and aquaria require thorough and regular cleaning to minimize problems of this nature.

◀ This Bearded Dragon has a malformed tall as a result of Metabolic Bone Disease (p. 119). The condition could be prevented by correct dietary supplementation during all stages of growth.

▲ **This Tree Frog has lost an eye but it is still able to lead an active life with this disability.**

SALMONELLOSIS

This disease can be transmitted from many pet animals to man (zoonosis) and vice versa. Salmonella is a genus of bacteria containing over 1500 species, many of which can cause food poisoning. In humans the symptoms are nausea, vomiting and diarrhea, and in severe cases it may even cause death.

Most salmonella infections are a result of poor human food hygiene. Raw chicken is a commonly-infected meat and raw egg is another potential offender.

Many pet animals such as hamsters, rabbits and more exotic species, can be symptom-less carriers of these bacteria, with no infection ever occurring. Any animal with symptoms of diarrhea, nausea and sudden weight loss should be examined.

Infected animals should be treated. The source of infection needs to be identified and eliminated; the culprits are usually old food or dirty caging.

Do not worry unnecessarily about salmonella. Providing you heed normal animal/human hygiene procedures – washing hands with a micro-bactericidal soap, never cleaning animal housing or equipment in the same area that is used for food preparation, always disinfecting equipment and housing on a regular basis – you have little to worry about.

Follow basic hygiene rules. Keep animals off furniture and out of kitchens. Clean the housing and furnishings on a regular basis with a 10% chlorine solution. After contact with any animal, wash your hands. Ordinary soap is a poor cleanser so use a bactericidal soap, available from your pharmacist.

Glossary

A

Aestivation The act of passing the summer or dry season in a dormant state.

Amplexus A mating embrace seen in some amphibians.

Aquatic Growing, living, or found in water.

Arachnid A class of arthropods characterized by simple eyes and four pairs of legs, which includes spiders, scorpions, and ticks.

Arboreal Living above ground in trees or bushes.

Autonomy The ability to drop or shed the tail as a defense mechanism.

B

Brackish Water that is slightly briny or salty.

C

Carnivore Any animal or plant that feeds on animals; includes amphibians and snakes.

Casque A helmet-like structure.

CITES The Convention on International Trade in Endangered Species.

Cloaca The cavity into which the urinary, alimentary, and genital ducts open.

Crepuscular Predominantly active at dusk or before dawn.

D

Desiccate To dehydrate or dry out.

Dewlap Extendible flap of skin seen on some reptiles.

Diurnal Active during daylight hours.

Dysadysis The inability to perform ecdysis successfully (see Ecdysis).

E

Ecdysis The periodic shedding of the cuticle in insects and other arthropods and the outer skin layer in herptiles.

Ecosystem A system that combines interdependence upon and interaction between living organisms and the immediate environment.

Ectotherm Any animal that relies on external heat sources to maintain its body temperature.

Endoskeleton The internal structure, or skeleton, of a vertebrate animal.

Exoskeleton The external protective structure or cuticle of arthropods.

F

Fecal pellets Bodily waste matter discharged through the anus.

G

Gonopods The paired external reproductive organs of some insects and arthropods.

Gravid Pregnant.

H

Hemipenes The paired reproductive organ of a male reptile.

Herbivore An animal that feeds on plant matter.

Hermaphrodite Possessing both male and female reproductive organs.

Herpetologist One who studies amphibians and reptiles.

Herptile Any reptile or amphibian.

Hibernate To pass the winter in a dormant state with a reduced metabolic rate.

Humidity The moisture content of air.

Hygrometer An instrument used to measure humidity.

I

Instar The developmental stage of an insect that occurs between any two molts.
Invertebrate Any animal lacking a backbone.

M

Metamorphosis Rapid transformation of a larva into an adult—i.e., tadpole to frog.

N

Neotony The term used to describe the reproductive ability of amphibians that still possess larval characteristics.
Nocturnal Active mainly at night.
Nymph The larval stage of some insects.

O

Omnivore Any animal that feeds upon both plants and animals.
Ootheca A capsule containing eggs.
Oviparous Producing eggs that hatch outside the female's body.
Ovipositor The egg-laying organ of many female insects.

P

Parotid gland A toxin-producing gland in amphibians.
Parthenogenesis A reproductive process whereby the egg can develop without being fertilized.
Phase The term used to describe a variation in the normal form or color of an animal brought about by seasonal or geographic change.
Prehensile Adapted for grasping or wrapping around an object.

S

Sexually dimorphic The ability to differentiate between the sexes by external physical features.
Slough Any outer covering that is shed, such as the dead outer layer of the skin of a snake.
Spermatophore A jelly-like capsule of sperm.
Spiracles Respiratory apertures of insects.

T

Taxonomy The science of classification of living things.
Terrestrial Any animal or plant living on the land.
Territorial A pattern of behavior used to defend a specific area.
Thermoregulation A method used by ectotherms to maintain optimum body temperature by moving between environments of different temperatures.
Thermostat An instrument used to maintain a set temperature.

U

Ultraviolet (UV) light The part of the electro-magnetic spectrum that consists of wavelengths shorter than light and longer than X-rays. UVA (320–400nm) and UVB (260–320nm) are essential for many herptiles. UVC (200–260nm) is dangerous to living organisms.

V

Vent The external opening of the urinary and genital systems.
Vermiculite Expanded mica used as a bedding or incubating medium.
Vertebrate Any animal with a bony skeleton, including all reptiles and amphibians.
Vivarium An enclosure for herptiles and invertebrates.

Useful Information

CLUBS AND SOCIETIES

There are a number of clubs and societies that you may wish to join. They are an excellent source of information about all aspects of the natural history and maintenance of exotic species and they are one way to contact like-minded individuals and to obtain livestock. There are also many reptile shows, open to the public, which are advertised in journals and club newsletters.

International Tortoise and Turtle Society
Route 3
Box 328
Big Pine Key, FL 33043

National Tortoise and Turtle Society
P.O. Box 66935
Phoenix, AZ 85082

New York Herpetological Society
P.O. Box 1245
Grand Central Station
New York, NY 10163-1245

Society for the Study of Amphibians and Reptiles
Department of Zoology
Miami University
Oxford, OH 45046

Varanid Information Exchange
8726D S. Sepulveda Boulevard
#243
Los Angeles, CA 90045

MAGAZINES

Copeia
American Society of Icythyologists and Herpetologists
810 East 10 Street
P.O. Box 1897
Lawrence, KS 66044

Reptile and Amphibian
RD 3
Box 3709-A
Pottsville, PA 17901

Reptiles Magazine
P.O. Box 6050
Mission Viejo, CA 92690

Vivarium
Vivarium Publishing Group
P.O. Box 300067
Escondido, CA 92030
Email: www.thevivarium.com
Published six times a year and available on subscription or at specialist pet stores. This is one of the best publications currently available on the subject.

FURTHER READING

Arnold, E.J. & Burton, A.J., *A Field Guide to the Reptiles and Amphibians of Britain and Europe.* London: HarperCollins, 1996.

Bartlett, R.D. & Patricia, *Corn Snakes and Other Rat Snakes: A Complete Pet Owner's Manual.* Hauppauge: Barron's Educational Series, Inc., 1996.

Bartlett, R.D. & Patricia, *Iguanas: A Complete Pet Owner's Manual.* Hauppauge: Barron's Educational Series, Inc., 1995.

Bartlett, R.D. & Patricia, *Monitors, Tegus, and Related Lizards: A Complete Pet Owner's Manual.* Hauppauge: Barron's Educational Series, Inc., 1996.

Bartlett, R.D. & Patricia, *Turtles and Tortoises: A Complete Pet Owner's Manual.* Hauppauge: Barron's Educational Series, Inc., 1996.

de Vosjoli, Phillipe, *General Care and Maintenance of Leopard Geckos.* Santee: Advanced Vivarium Systems, 1990.

de Vosjoli, Phillipe, *Lizard Keeper's Handbook.* Santee: Advanced Vivarium Systems, 1990.

Ferguson, G. & de Vosjoli, Phillipe, *Care and Breeding Panther, Veiled, and Parsons Chameleons.* Santee: Advanced Vivarium Systems, 1995.

Indiviglio, Frank, *Newts and Salamanders: A Complete Pet Owner's Manual.* Hauppauge: Barron's Educational Series, Inc., 1996.

Jes, Harald, *Lizards in the Terrarium.* Hauppauge: Barron's Educational Series, Inc., 1987.

Schultz, Stanley A. & Marguerite J., *The Tarantula Keeper's Guide.* Hauppauge: Barron's Educational Series, Inc., 1998.

Wagner, Doug, *Boas: A Complete Pet Owner's Manual.* Hauppauge: Barron's Educational Series, Inc., 1996.

Index

Major entries are indicated by
bold page numbers

A

abscesses, 119
Acheta domestica, 19
acquiring a pet, 8–10
aestivation, 46
Agalychnis callidryas, 42–43
ailments, 118–121
allergy, 10
Ambystoma mexicanum, 26–29
  tigrinum, 35
amphibia, 22–43
  bacterial infection, 120
  classification, 25
Anole, Brown, **53**
  Green, **52–53**
Anolis carolinensis, 52–53
  sagrei, 53
Anopheles sp., 98
Apis sp., 98
aquarium, design, 12–14
  establishing, 8
  filter, 16
Artemia sp., 20
Avicularia avicularia, 113
Axolotl, 9, 20, 25, **26–29**

B

bacterial infection, 120
Bearded Dragon, 13, 15, 18,
  54–55, 120
Beetle, Colorado, 98
benefits of keeping pets, 10
bites, 9

blisters, causes, 119
Bombina orientalis, 32–33
bowl, water, 15
Brachypelma albopilosa, 110
  smithi, 115
breeding, triggering, 39, 41
Bufo marinus, 33

C

Carausius morosus, 100–101
cascillia, 25
Chamaeleo calyptratus, 60–63
  pardalis, 62
Chameleon, American, 52
  Panther, **62**
  requirements for keeping, 9
  Veiled, 13, 15, 18, **60–63**
Chicobolus spinigerus, 105
CITES, 7
classification, amphibia, 25
  invertebrate, 99
  reptile, 47
conservation, 6–7
  habitat loss, 6, 25, 37
cricket, as food, 19
  house, 19

D

Dabb Lizard, 64
daphnia, 20
dehydration, 119
desiccation, 119
diary, pet, 11
disease, control, 120–122
  metabolic bone, 13, 119, 120
  salmonellosis, 121
Dragons, Bearded, 13, 15, 18,
  54–55, 120
Drosophila sp., 19

E

earthworm, as food, 20
ecdysis, 119
ectotherm, definition, 98
Elaphe guttata guttata, 84–87
Epibolus sp., 104–105
Eublepharis macularius, 48–51
Eurycantha calcarata, 100
euthanasia, 120

F

food, 18–21
  refusal to feed, 21
  supplements, 21
Frog, African Clawed, 20, **30–31**
  Common, 24
  Dwarf Clawed, **31**
  lighting requirements, 14
  see also Tree Frog
fruit flies, 19

G

Gecko, Day, **51**
  Leopard, 7, 9, **48–51**, 118
gerbil, as food, 21
Grammostola cala, 111
Gryllus sp., 19

H

handling, amphibians, 11
  invertebrates, 11
  lizards, 11
  snakes, 11
  tarantulas, 111–112
health, maintaining, 118–121
heating, 8–9, **13–15**
  ceramic, 15